Through fatherly wisdom and practical guidance, Larry passionately and respectfully validates the function of micro churches. Composed from biblical, historical, and global perspectives, *Micro Church Networks* offers comprehensive as well as relevant and timely counsel for those who oversee, lead, explore, or initiate this form of church.

Keith Yoder, Founder, Teaching the Word Ministries

God is birthing new wineskins in the form of micro churches all over the world. Larry Kreider makes a strong case for this model in our current times. These churches carry the essence of New Testament Christianity in a format that is easy to lead, and most importantly, easy to multiply. Larry shows how these churches can remain healthy through being connected in a network. As we stand on the threshold of a massive global harvest of the lost, this important book is an inspiring yet practical handbook for those wanting to plant micro churches.

Dr. Barry L. Wissler, President, HarvestNet International, Pennsylvania

Micro Church Networks

A church for a
new generation

LARRY KREIDER

House to House Publications
Lititz, PA USA

Some of the content of this book is adapted from Larry Kreider's book *House Church Networks: A church for a new generation* (2001) published by House to House Publications. Much has changed since that initial publication. This edition, *Micro Church Networks*, provides a current perspective on the growth of micro church networks worldwide as well as field-tested practical insights for establishing healthy biblical micro church networks in any culture.

Micro Church Networks: A church for a new generation
© 2020 DOVE International

Published by
House to House Publications
11Toll Gate Road
Lititz, Pennsylvania 17543 USA
Tele: 800-848-5892
www.h2hp.com

ISBN 13: 978-1-7357388-0-2

Unless otherwise noted, all scripture quotations in this publication are taken from the *Holy Bible, New International Version* (NIV).
© 1973, 1978, 1984 by International Bible Society. Used by permission of Zondervan Publishing House. All rights reserved.

Printed in the United States of America

Dedication

To our Lord Jesus Christ, the author and finisher of our faith, and to the next generation of Christian leaders whose sole purpose in life is to know Jesus Christ, obey His voice and desire to please Him while modeling church life according to the pattern of the New Testament.

Acknowledgements

A special word of thanks goes to Diane Omondi, my editor, who tirelessly helped me to write this manuscript. Thank you, Sarah Sauder, for coordinating the project. Another grateful thanks is extended to proofreaders.

I also wish to express my appreciation to the DOVE International family worldwide for their openness to the Holy Spirit as He continues to lead us and the rest of the body of Christ into our Lord's purposes during these strategic days.

CONTENTS

1. There's a New Church Emerging...........................9
2. God is Preparing New Wineskins.....................18
3. A Biblical Vision for Micro Churches 25
4. Community Churches, Megachurches
    and Micro Churches 33
5. Our Story: Community Church to Megachurch
    to the New Micro Churches...............................43
6. The Growth of Micro Churches Globally.........48
7. The Role of Spiritual Fathers and Mothers:
    Make Disciples..60
8. Learning from History.......................................73
9. Simplicity and Unity 79
10. Planting and Leading a Micro Church 90
11. Healthy Micro Church Meetings.....................101
12. The Nuts and Bolts of Micro Church Multiplication.....116
13. Modern Day Micro Church Networks 125
14. A New Model for a New Time..........................135
15. Broadening our Scope 141

Appendix A: Questions Most Often Asked
About Micro Church Networks..............................145
Appendix B: What is DOVE International?.............150
Appendix C: Recommended Reading 160

CHAPTER 1

There's a
New Church Emerging!

God never tires of releasing fresh waves of revival on His people. God told Isaiah, "See I am doing a new thing. Do you not perceive it?" (Isaiah 43:19).

I believe micro churches are a new move of God for the present season in his Kingdom. Are we able to perceive what God is doing?

Micro churches provide a fresh and flexible structure for the invigorating flow of God's Spirit. This "new" form of church life is actually not new at all! It was the norm for New Testament believers and has been adopted through the centuries, particularly during times when God's people are facing persecution.

Micro church networks embrace community, accountability, and genuine faith. The model is soundly biblical and contemporarily viable. Micro churches include all the features of New Testament Christianity and at the same time satisfy the hunger for first-hand participation in community where believers learn by doing under the mentorship of spiritual fathers and mothers.

These groups are often called house churches because each one functions as a little church. They are networks because they work together to foster accountability and encouragement. I prefer to use the term micro church networks to identify this inspiring flow of God's Spirit.

I am very excited to observe and participate in the fresh, divine expression of micro church networks. I believe these networks will continue to multiply in North America as they have been doing in other nations. Places like China, central Asia, Latin America, India and Cambodia have experienced tremendous church growth through micro churches that disciple and empower every member for the work of ministry.

The definition of the church of the New Testament was actually the people who were set apart and called to faith in Christ. Believers did not go to church or join the church; they were the church. All members functioned as priests because everyone served as a minister. Each person was given on-the-job-training and learned how to make disciples. These followers of Christ practiced their faith in spiritual families, met in homes and radically changed their world. They grew in number as they obeyed God's Word and shared resources and spiritual blessings. They multiplied into more and more groups of believers meeting in homes, all networking together.

Micro church networks are now multiplying rapidly throughout North America and in many nations: China, India, Kenya, Myanmar, Peru, Germany and many more. They are growing both in numbers and influence. They provide an alternative form of church life that many are seeking.

The constant need for new wineskins

The New Testament records a conversation Jesus had with followers of John the Baptist about how to respond when things are being done in a new way among God's people. More specifically, John's disciples were concerned that Jesus and His disciples were not following the rules of the Law of Moses about fasting. Jesus said, "And no one pours new wine into old wineskins. If he does, the new wine will burst the skins, the wine will run out and the wineskins will be ruined. No, new wine must be poured into new wineskins" (Luke 5:37-38).

I have noticed that new Christians are like new wine, still in the process of fermentation. Putting them into old wineskins (existing church structures) could lead to incompatibility. The new wineskin of micro churches might concern some believers who, perhaps without realizing it, equate Christianity with the structures and expressions they are familiar with.

Although there are already thousands upon thousands of healthy, vibrant churches around the world, new wineskins are continually needed to accommodate believers who do not fit into the existing church structures. Micro churches are helping restore the simplicity of the New Testament church.

I had the privilege of serving as senior pastor of a church for fifteen years. Started in 1980, our rural church plant in south central Pennsylvania grew from twenty-five people to over one thousand within seven years. By 1990, we had grown to well over two thousand members. It was truly a miracle of grace. Back then, we thought we had a radical outlook on doing church because we established small groups as our foundational structure. However, after several years, it became apparent that there was a sense of unrest in our growing church.

I especially noticed this among some of the young people. They craved a more flexible format for church. They were saying the same kinds of things we had said ten years earlier: "We are looking for something new. We need something that truly meets our needs." Our ten-year-old wineskin had begun to age—it was past its prime for some in the younger generation.

It didn't take long to conclude that we needed to find ways of planting new churches (new wineskins) and begin the process of handing over the reins to the next generation. If we didn't, we would lose what we already had. How then could we reach out to our world and reap a harvest? As Dr. Peter Wagner said so often, "The single most effective way to evangelize is to plant new churches."[1]

In order to penetrate society effectively, it is suggested that one church is needed for every five hundred to one thousand people.[2] The influence of house churches can support more traditional church models to provide enough churches and church options for our population.

Lorin Smith, writing about micro churches in Bermuda's daily newspaper *The Royal Gazette*, says this:

> A largely hidden, yet growing phenomenon is changing
> the face of Christianity in the West and profoundly affecting
> the way in which Christians are choosing to practice their

faith…. Thousands of Christians across America, Australia, Canada, New Zealand and the United Kingdom are gathering in homes to study the Scriptures together, pray, share the Lord's Supper and experience the fellowship and simplicity of first century Christianity.[3]

"Yes, we are right now in the midst of the early days of a sovereign, very radical, move of God," says Nate Krupp, publisher of the book *God's Simple Plan for His Church*. "We are seeing God do incredible things: people are leaving the institutional church by the thousands… they long to use their giftings to serve God and see 'the priesthood of all believers,' instead of 'the clergy,' and they long to see the Holy Spirit allowed to freely move."[4]

As new micro churches network together, thousands of new churches can be planted rapidly throughout the nations of the world. Many more new churches are needed to care for the harvest of souls coming into God's kingdom.

Smaller groups provide a niche among both young and old

It is not just the younger generation that backs away from full participation in church life because they do not feel needed in the larger crowd. Middle aged and older people, too, are looking for a new model of church where they can be fully involved. I can still vividly remember a man in his late 50's confiding in me, with tears running down his cheeks, after I taught at his megachurch. He said, "I know the Lord called me years ago to be a pastor, but I just do not know how it can ever happen here in my church."

This man, who put a high priority on relationships, was a loving person with a pastor's heart. He was longing to fulfill God's call on his life. Think what could happen if he had the opportunity to be involved in a micro church. As a spiritual father in a micro church, he could fulfill his heart's cry. In a micro church, he could look after his extended spiritual family and find his niche.

While micro churches do not appeal to everyone in the younger generation, I believe Christians who are younger will often take the lead in starting new micro churches and networks. Why? Because they will thrive in a new wineskin that fits their generation's need for authentic relationships. Young adults are very open to small groups that are based on friendships and socializing. They love to spend time in homes and in discussion. This young generation especially craves real-life connections because it is a generation raised in the communication patterns of the internet and social media that often lack physical, personal connections:

> Our culture, once based exclusively on physical contact, is being transformed to one where goods and services are accessible without face-to-face contact with other people. Technology enables this transformation....[5]

Although social media creates an online community with Facebook, Instagram, newsgroups and the ability to run a business merely through an online presence, physical human contact is a vital missing element. Technology and all its helpful gadgets do not inspire deep relational connections. People are looking for dependable, meaningful, personal relationships.

God wants to connect the generations

In addition to a connection with their peers, young people are looking for significant interaction with the older generations. They desire to walk with spiritual fathers and mothers who will come alongside them, encourage them, and support their dreams and efforts.

God longs to connect the generations in healthy relationships so they can work together in unity and oneness to advance His kingdom. In the book, *The Cry for Spiritual Fathers and Mothers*, I explain it like this:

> God's intention is to raise spiritual parents who are willing to nurture spiritual children and help them grow in their Christian lives. This is a fulfillment of the Lord's promise in the last days to "turn the hearts of the fathers to the children, and the hearts of the children to their fathers..." (Malachi 4:6).

> The Lord wants to restore harmony among fathers and their children, both naturally and spiritually, so fathers can

freely impart their inheritance to the next generation…. With the old and the young working together, a mighty and ongoing spiritual legacy will multiply and endure. Imparting spiritual fatherhood fills the void and closes the gap of broken relationships between the old and the young.[6]

The generations must learn to work together. The heart's cry of the older generation must be to release the younger generation to fulfill the Lord's call.

I remember when Dan Yutzy, a church leader and professor from Taylor University, was addressing a group of Mennonite bishops in Lancaster County, Pennsylvania forty years ago. Speaking about the younger leadership represented, he said: "We must release these young men and let them go!" He knew the next generation needed to be trusted to start new church structures to accommodate the new followers of Christ. I was a product of this decision. The young believers we discipled who came to Christ through friendship evangelism were not fitting into the churches in our community. These churches had traditions and expectations the new Christians could not relate to. It became apparent that a new structure was needed in which these new believers could thrive.

Each generation needs to find its fit

Every generation needs to be free to discover and discern which wineskin is best for them. I like the way Leonard Sweet explains it in his book, *Aqua Church:*

> My wife is a tea drinker. Her favorite container is a little cup with a handle so tiny I can't even get my finger through it. My favorite container is a Jadite coffee mug (I started collecting Fire King Jadite long before Martha Stewart inflated the market and made it uncollectible). Our eight-year-old Thane's favorite container is a little glass we put juice in. Our three-year-old Soren's favorite container is a Winnie-the-Pooh sippy cup. Eighteen-month-old Egil's favorite container is a bottle.
>
> Every generation needs a shape that fits its own hands— its own soul. Each generation, every person, needs a different

handle from which to receive the living waters of Jesus. Our task is to pour the living water into anything that anyone will pick up.

By "anything," I mean that literally: anything. If I want to reach my twenty-second century children (they probably will live to see 2100) with the gospel of Jesus, I must be prepared to pour the living water into containers of which I myself would never be caught dead drinking. This is what Paul meant when he talked about our "becoming all things to all men" that we might win some (1 Corinthians 9:22).[7]

Once again, the generation of today needs a unique "shape that fits its hands." They need to be released to find that shape.

After speaking at a leadership conference at a large church in the United States, a woman said to me, "Every week, my home is filled with young people, mostly in their twenties. They are not the kind of kids that fit in the traditional church. I know they are experiencing church right in my home, but I do not want to compete with my church or be misunderstood. However, I see that we are becoming the church as a body of believers." Many others face this same dilemma. They are experiencing dynamic church life in a home, but need to be released to really be the church.

A new wineskin is emerging that could change the way church life looks today. God is preparing a new wineskin so the new and the old can work together to advance His kingdom. Let's not resist it.

Find a way "back to the future"

A popular science fiction film called *Back to the Future* tells the story of a young man who was accidentally sent back in time. In the past, he learns vital information for the future, but must find a way to get "back to the future" intact.

Perhaps we should take a step back in time to learn from the New Testament church to help us solve some of our modern-day church dilemmas. As we learn about micro churches, we have an excellent pattern to follow from the New Testament.

Soon after Pentecost when the Holy Spirit fell on those gathered in an upper room, many Jews who were in Jerusalem were coming to faith in Jesus Christ on a daily basis. Acts 2:41 says that after Peter addressed the crowd, giving an explanation from the Old Testament about the pouring out of God's Spirit and the resurrection of Jesus, "those who accepted his message were baptized, and about three thousand were added to their number that day."

In other words, the number of believers jumped from the 120 who were in the upper room to over three thousand. How could these new Christians possibly be taken care of? What wineskin could contain this exponential growth? The methodology used by the first disciples is described like this: "So continuing daily with one accord in the temple, and breaking bread from house to house, they ate their food with gladness and simplicity of heart, praising God and having favor with all the people. And the Lord added to the church daily those who were being saved" (Acts 2:46-47 NKJV).

The believers met together in homes as well as in the temple. "They devoted themselves to the apostles' teaching and to the fellowship, to the breaking of bread and to prayer" (Acts 2:42). As they ministered to one another and listened to teaching from the apostles, their numbers kept increasing.

The pattern of meeting in small groups in the homes of believers continued throughout the life of the early church. Paul refers again to this practice in Acts 20:20 when he declares to the believers in Ephesus, "…I have not hesitated to preach anything that would be helpful to you but have taught you publicly and from house to house." We see evidence of small home groups—actually micro churches—among believers in Ephesus, Rome and Philippians as well.

This is further explained in my book, *House to House*:

> The letter that Paul wrote to the Christians in Rome was written to believers in Jesus Christ who met in people's homes. In his letter to the Romans, Paul indicates that one of these groups met in the house of Priscilla and Aquila (see Romans 16:3-5). Paul also sent his greeting to the house of Aristobulus

and the household of Narcissus (see Romans 16:10-11). When Paul wrote to his friend Philemon, he expressed his greeting to the church in his house, "...To Philemon our dear friend and fellow workers, to Appius our sister, to Archippus our fellow soldier and to the church that meets in your home" (Philippians 1:1-2).

Periodically, down through the ages, the church has lost the New Testament component of meeting in small groups in homes of individual believers and has placed an emphasis on the church as it meets in larger buildings....

We believe the Lord wants us to get back to seeing the church as people, not as a place where believers meet each weekend. Our homes, places of business, schools and other circles of contact provide excellent places for the church to meet as we infiltrate our spheres of influence with the Good News.[8]

The book of Proverbs tells us, "My child, don't lose sight of good planning and insight. Hang on to them. For they will fill you with life and bring you honor and respect" (Proverbs 3:21-22 NLT). For thousands of believers throughout the world, God's plan might very well include involvement in a micro church network. The Lord will lead us step by step.

Notes

1 C. Peter Wagner, *Church Planting for a Greater Harvest*, (Ventura, CA: Regal Books, 1990), p. 11

2 Jim Montgomery, *DAWN 2000: 7 Million Churches to Go*, (Littleton, CO: William Carey Publishing, 1989).

3 Lorin Smith, "The House Church Movement," http://housechurch.org/basics/lorin_smith.html

4 Nate Krupp, www.radchr.net

5 Carole Agnes, et. al, "Transformation to Virtual Societies: Forces and Issues," Information Society, Vol 14 No 2, March 1998.

6 Larry Kreider, *The Cry for Spiritual Fathers and Mothers*, (Lititz, PA: House to House Publications, 2000), pp. 3,4

7 Leonard Sweet, *Aqua Church*, (Loveland, CO: Group Publishing, 1999), pp. 28-29

8 Larry Kreider, *House to House*, (Lititz, PA: House to House Publications, 2014), pp. 50-51

CHAPTER 2

God is Preparing
New Wineskins

Micro church networks are gaining momentum both in North America and around the world. The new wineskin of micro churches that is emerging could be called a new Reformation because it will radically change the look of church as we know it. These churches that meet in homes are actual churches, not just Bible studies or small groups. They are changing the way we understand church.

We must change the way we "do church"

In his book, *Boiling Point*, George Barna takes an in-depth look at the changing beliefs and attitudes of society today and how Christians must anticipate the world's spiritual needs. One of the innovations he suggests is "doing church" in a way that will restore community and authenticity to the church:

> Popular in other countries, especially Southeast Asia, thousands of independent faith groups will meet for a complete church experience and expression within living rooms and garages...this option will appeal to individuals who are especially interested in restoring authenticity, community and simplicity to the church.[1]

Barna's extensive studies of the pervading culture cause him to suggest that the gaping deficiencies of today's church prevent her from fulfilling the needs of today's generation. There seems to be an uncommon courage on the young generation today. Known as "Generation Z," these young people are part of a universal culture. All around the world, these young people have similar ways of thinking. With the global media beaming the same message to the same generation worldwide, young people from diverse cultures around the globe are more the same in their thinking today than ever before.

Members of Generation Z genuinely believe they can change the world. With the capacities of the internet and social media, every individual now has a voice. Their greatest desire is to make a difference and bring change for good, not necessarily to make money or become famous.

The younger generation is asking a lot of questions. They are quick to challenge the status quo. They want to solve the problems they see around them. Generation Z has grown up in a world where a package ordered online is expected to be on their doorstep within two days—or, for a small additional cost, the very next morning! Generation Z sees the world through the eyes of endless possibilities. So when a member of Generation Z confronts a problem of systemic injustice in society, it bothers them. The thinking is, "If a package can arrive at my door in two days, then why is homelessness still pervasive in my city?" This is commonly how someone from Generation Z would view the world. The attitude is, "anything is possible." They do not settle for doing things the way things have been done before, but are looking for answers to the problems they see around them. This includes a quest for fresh expressions of faith that are relevant to their modern lives.

Let me emphasize that although micro church networks appeal to many who are young, thousands of people from all generations have the same needs and desires for a fresh expression of their faith. Many are in a "research and development" stage regarding starting new micro churches in our generation.

According to Barna, nine percent of adults in the United States, approximately twenty million people, attend a house church (micro church) in a typical week. That more than doubles to forty-three million who attend a house church (micro church) in a typical month.[2]

Small micro churches are expanding rapidly because they meet a desperate need in church life today.

Before we take a closer look at this growing, worldwide grassroots movement of micro church networks, we need to clarify an important point. Micro churches should not be confused with the small group-based church model or with cell group-based churches.

How "cell churches" function

In the 1980s and 1990s, a new wineskin known as cell church started to flourish around the world. Many people realized traditional church methods were not meeting believers' needs. The church tended to be building-bound and clergy-centered. Many Christians longed for a place to belong and be used as effective witnesses to the gospel. Churches soon realized that small groups (cell groups) could help people rediscover that they could indeed "do the work of ministry." Left behind was a spectator mentality of church in which the pastor did all the work.

With the small group system made famous through David Yonggi Cho's massive church in South Korea, multitudes of cell churches emerged on the scene in many different denominations. Some churches started as new small group-based churches, other churches transitioned to small group-based ministry and still others simply developed small groups within their current church structure.

In the ensuing years, many churches utilized small groups that gave everyone a job to do. Everyone's talents and gifts were exercised to benefit others, and people were able to gain on-the-job training for leadership through hands-on experiences. These small groups also provided a more natural setting for evangelism since they gave the opportunity to do evangelism as a team. Together the group could pray for God to use them to reach each one's personal *oikos* (from the Greek word "household" in the Bible).

Our *oikos* are those people with whom we relate on a regular basis—our co-workers, family members, or those with whom we share a common interest such as sports or music. In a small group setting, non-believers are more easily drawn in and find a place to be loved and cared for. Today, nearly every denomination has some kind of small group structure that brings ministry and caring to a more personal level.

However, current small group-based churches continue to function mainly within the traditional church structure. In other words, although believers meet during the week in homes, these groups still function as complementary ministries to the larger Sunday church meeting. A senior pastor leads this larger gathering and also oversees the small group leaders. This structure of larger meetings and smaller group meetings involves many small group leaders, assistants and perhaps zone pastors, all of whom are accountable to the senior pastor and church leadership team. Additionally, a church with small groups needs to have a headquarters or a church building that accommodates various church functions.

How micro churches function

Micro churches are entirely different from this. Although they meet in homes like small groups, that's where most of the similarities end. Unlike the small group-based church or community church with cell groups, each micro church is meant to be a complete church on its own. They have elders, they collect tithes and offerings, and the leadership is responsible before the Lord for the souls of the people in the micro church according to the spiritual responsibility described in Hebrews 13:17.

Each church is led not by a group leader and a team of assistant leaders, but rather by a spiritual father or mother who functions as the lead elder along with a small eldership team. He or she does not simply lead a meeting in a house, but rather provides an environment for people to grow spiritually in the context of everyday life. There is no need for a church building in which to meet because each micro church is a fully functioning church in itself, meeting in a home, office, restaurant or other suitable location.

This is not to say that a micro church consists of only one group. A micro church should encourage smaller groups within the group that meet for prayer, encouragement and accountability, often outside of the actual micro church meeting. One small group of people could regularly meet for breakfast before work and another small group could meet to disciple new Christians in the micro church.

Each micro church, although a local church in itself, is committed to network with other micro churches in its city or region. This protects a micro church from pride, exclusiveness and heresy (more will be said about these inherent dangers of micro churches in chapter 12). Several micro church leaders I know tell me that their micro churches meet together once every month or so for corporate worship and teaching because they recognize the need to be connected. This desire to network comes from a similar desire to receive oversight from spiritual fathers and mothers in order to stay accountable. Our God is the God of the macro church and the God of the micro church. In Acts chapter 2, three thousand were baptized. They experienced macro church! But then they met in small micro churches and lived out their faith from house to house. There is a place for both macro church and micro church in the body of Christ.

I also find that many micro church leaders are intent on reproduction. Micro churches are relatively simple to start, provide a natural setting for ministry, and are easily replicated. They provide a relevant way to engage our communities with the claims of Jesus. When they outgrow the house or place where they are meeting, instead of constructing a church building, they plant a new micro church. It sounds a bit like the book of Acts, doesn't it?

Like the New Testament church, the micro church network focuses on relationships, reaching the lost and raising spiritual fathers and mothers in-house who serve and care for their spiritual family. The micro church emerges as a fluid and flexible church.

What a healthy micro church is not

Part of understanding what micro churches look like is understanding the 'flip side'—what a healthy micro church should not look like. First of all, a healthy micro church is not a group of people who are disgruntled with the community church or megachurch. Second, a micro church is not an ingrown club of people who have forgotten the harvest. Third, it is not Christians who are independent, do not believe in spiritual authority and are unwilling to submit to recognized leaders within the body of Christ. Fourth, healthy micro church networks are not comprised of groups of people who have been together for a number of years and have only slightly grown in size or have not grown at all.

Don't isolate! Find that connection

I meet many believers, especially in North America, who have spent the past twenty to thirty years with a sense of unrest in their spirits. They love the Lord, but are discouraged. A couple of decades ago, they experienced a new wave of the Spirit. They envisioned a radical New Testament church experience emerging from this spiritual renewal. But cumbersome church structures and traditional church meetings and procedures frustrated the dream. Now they find themselves in a "holding pattern." They dream of experiencing life-changing discipleship that transforms society around them, but are not experiencing anything close to it.

Deep in their spirits, they believe the Lord is about to make some radical changes in His church. They have been looking for something new, yet are not even sure what they are looking for. They are passionately in love with Jesus, but feel unable to find their niche in the body of Christ.

Some have become disillusioned. Others have been hurt or are even bitter toward the church, feeling they are right and the rest of the church is wrong. They meet in their homes with like-minded believers, cut off from the rest of the body of Christ. To make matters worse, there are entire books written advocating this type of unwholesome behavior.

We must "beware of those who live in anger toward the established church," says Ralph Moore who is responsible for planting hundreds of Hope Chapel churches throughout Hawaii and the west coast of the United States. "The anger of man still can't work the righteousness of God."[3] I totally agree.

Micro churches, and churches of any kind, should never be exclusive entities cut off from the rest of the body of Christ. A simple litmus test to discern if a micro church is healthy is this: does the church focus on loving the Lord, loving each other, reaching the lost and loving the rest of the body of Christ?

Jesus "came to seek and to save what was lost" (Luke 19:10) and He prayed that we would be one as the Father and the Son are one (John 17:21). Healthy believers will want to relate closely to the rest of the body of Christ because they want to be one with the Father and each other.

God offers a richness through different Christian faith expressions. Each kind of church contributes its strengths to the others. We need each other. God uses different types of churches to accomplish His purposes. Each part of the church, regardless of denominational labels or structure, is a vital part of the body of Christ. God works through all His people.

In the next chapter, we will look more at the church in the New Testament to see what we can learn about church life that fits our generation.

Notes

1   Lisa Cannon Green/Lifeway, "Study: Thousands of Churches Closing Every Year but There Is a Silver Lining," www.charismanews.com/us/53715, December 9, 2015

2   George Barna and Mark Hatch, *Boiling Point*, (Ventura, CA: Regal Books, 2001), p. 250

3   House2House Magazine, March 2001, p. 20

CHAPTER 3

A Biblical Vision
for Micro Churches

As I mentioned in the first chapter, the letter that Paul wrote to the Christians in Rome was written to believers in Jesus Christ who met in peoples' homes. In his letter to the Romans, Paul indicates that one of these groups met in the home of Priscilla and Aquila. "Greet Priscilla and Aquila, my fellow workers in Christ Jesus, who risked their own necks for my life, to whom not only I give thanks, but also all the churches of the Gentiles. Likewise greet the church that is in their house" (Romans 16:3-5).

Paul also sent his greetings to the household of Aristobulus and the household of Narcissus (Romans 16:10-11). When Paul wrote to his friend Philemon, he expressed his greetings to the church in his house, ". . . to the beloved Apphia, Archippus our fellow soldier, and to the church in your house" (Philemon 1:2).

Periodically, down through the ages, the church has lost the New Testament component of meeting in believers' homes and has placed an emphasis on the church as it meets in large buildings. In his book *The Open Church*, James H. Rutz explains it like this:

> It was in 323 AD, almost three hundred years after the birth of the church, that Christians first met in something we now call a 'building.' For all three hundred years before that, the church met in living rooms!

> Constantine built these assembly buildings for Christians not only in Constantinople, but also in Rome, Jerusalem, and in many parts of Italy, all between 323 and 327 A.D. This trig-

gered a massive "church building" fad in large cities all over the Empire.[1]

Temple ministry is beneficial for corporate worship, teaching and celebration, but I believe the Lord wants us to see the church as people, not as a place where believers meet. Our homes, places of business, schools, coffee shops, and other places of contact provide ideal meeting places as we infiltrate our spheres of influence with the gospel of Jesus Christ.

What was the early church really like?

T.L. Osborne, in his book, *Soul-winning, Out Where the Sinners Are* tells the story of a possible conversation with Aquila in Ephesus, from the book of Acts:

"Good evening, Aquila. We understand you're a member of the church here. Could we come in and visit for a while?"

"Certainly. Come in."

"If you don't mind, we would like for you to tell us about the way the churches here in Asia Minor carry on their soul-winning program. We read that you have been a member of a church in Corinth and Rome, as well as this one here in Ephesus. You should be very qualified to tell us about evangelism in the New Testament Church. If you don't mind, we'd like to visit your church while we're here."

"Sit down, you're already in the church. It meets in my home."

"You don't have a church building?"

"What's a church building? No, I guess we don't."

"Tell me Aquila, what is your church doing to evangelize Ephesus? What are you doing to reach the city with the gospel?"

"Oh, we already evangelized Ephesus. Every person in the city clearly understands the Gospel . . . We just visited every home in the city. That's the way the church in Jerusalem first evangelized that city (Acts 5:42). The disciples there evangelized the entire city of Jerusalem in a very short time. All the other churches in Asia Minor have followed that example."[2]

The church of today should take a lesson from the early church. Churches are trying to reach people for Christ with extravagant church programs and 21st century methodology. While such methods have their place, they can never be a substitute for personal relationships formed in the context of genuine Christian community.

Living stones

The Bible calls us "living stones." This is found in I Peter 2:4-5: "Coming to Him as to a living stone, rejected indeed by men, but chosen by God and precious, you also, as living stones, are being built up a spiritual house, a holy priesthood, to offer up spiritual sacrifices acceptable to God through Jesus Christ."

Each believer has been made alive through faith in our Lord Jesus Christ. The Lord builds us together with other Christians into a type of spiritual house or community. Christianity is practical. The New Testament church met relationally from house to house. They were "living stones" built together by relationship into a spiritual house. Many churches today focus on their larger Sunday meetings. They sometimes look more like a pile of stones dumped at a church building each Sunday morning rather than living stones that are built together into a spiritual house through God-given relationships. Micro churches, because they are smaller, can focus more on relational Christianity.

As "living stones," we can demobilize the devil as we obey the living God. Imagine a large stone wall made up of thousands of stones mortared together. These thousands of stones are comprised of clusters of stones that touch one another. Can you imagine how frightening it would be if each of these stones were alive and they all decided to walk toward you at the same time? That could be how the devil feels when, as Christians, we pull together and obey the prompting of the Holy Spirit to build together by relationship and destroy the works of darkness.

Each living stone can only touch a few other living stones at one time. This picture represents believers who are knit together in small groups through relationships as they are united in the Lord. Ten people who are of one mind and heart can have a tremendous impact on the kingdom of darkness. The devil would like to separate us, isolate us, and leave us without the support of our brothers and sisters in Christ.

In small groups and micro churches, we can interact meaningfully with a few other people, both those who are born again and those who are not yet saved, through encouragement, prayer, and practical service. As each micro church obeys our Lord Jesus, we will have a powerful effect on our communities. It is important to remember that the "ministers" Paul speaks about in the New Testament are not only the pastors or leaders—they include all the saints (believers). We are all called to minister to and with the 'stones' that we are touching in God's spiritual house.

Tradition, Tradition!

Tevye, the patriarch in the classic motion picture, The Fiddler on the Roof, loved tradition. If something has worked in the past, most people, like Tevye, are happy to continue on in the same way. The old adage, "If it isn't broken, it doesn't need to be fixed," satisfies many Christians today as they continue on in known patterns of church structure.

In DOVE International, we see ourselves called to an "underground church movement." We are set up in a nontraditional structure of small groups (sometimes called cell groups, life groups or discipleship groups) and micro churches networking together. In our desire to be patterned after the New Testament church, we have deviated from traditional church structure. Yet, most congregations in the DOVE International family have conceded in at least one way to the tradition around us, namely that of gathering every Sunday morning.

Church history tells us that the believers met on the first day of the week. But since the emphasis was on house to house ministry, and they didn't have their own buildings until about 250 years later, it seems reasonable to assume that the believers met in homes on Sundays.

We are not implying that it is wrong for congregations to meet in a building on a Sunday morning. Our culture is accustomed to Christians gathering in a church building every Sunday—there is nothing wrong with it at all. God has called and led many of us to do this. However, we need to ask ourselves why we meet together in this way. Is it because the Holy Spirit has led us to do so, or because it is dictated by tradition?

Don't misunderstand me. Not all tradition is wrong. Some traditions are godly and good. When traditions take on a life of their own, however, we may be in trouble, because we begin to trust a method rather than the Living God. Even small groups and micro churches can become legalistic and traditional if we trust the method rather than allowing God to keep us flexible and open to His leading.

The Jethro Principle

Moses as leader of the Israelite nation was quickly wearing himself out by continually listening to and solving the disputes and dilemmas which arose among the Israelites. He was weighed down by the responsibilities that came with serving more than three million people—who wouldn't be? The Israelites were disturbed because they had to wait day after day for Moses to hear their cases. This reminds me of many pastors today who are getting close to burnout as they try to juggle the crushing ministry responsibilities of their churches all by themselves.

Through Jethro, God gave Moses a simple solution so that he and the people would not be worn out. Able men were to be selected from among the people to listen to any problems which arose, solve the ones they could, and pass on the most difficult cases to Moses. This is explained in Exodus 18:21-24:

> Moreover you shall select from all the people able men, such as fear God, men of truth, hating covetousness; and place such over them to be rulers of thousands, rulers of hundreds, rulers of fifties, and rulers of tens. And let them judge the people at all times. Then it will be that every great matter they shall bring to you, but every small matter they themselves shall judge. So it will be easier for you, for they will bear the

burden with you. If you do this thing, and God so commands you, then you will be able to endure, and all this people will also go to their place in peace. So Moses heeded the voice of his father-in-law and did all that he had said.

There would be one judge for every one thousand people. Moses would appoint ten additional judges under him, each in charge of one hundred. Under each of them would be two judges, each responsible for the affairs of fifty people. Each of these would have five judges beneath him, each counseling ten persons. Only the most severe or perplexing problems would reach Moses.

It is not necessary to set up a legalistic system in the church that looks exactly like the structure Moses used. However, we need to see the church from God's perspective and use the wisdom He has given us in determining her structure. Our God set the sun and the moon and the stars in place; He is a God of order.

The early apostles understood the principle of delegation that Moses had used many years before. During the great revival that took place in the book of Acts, the apostles found it necessary to delegate authority and responsibility to others so that they could concentrate on their top priority—prayer and the ministry of the Word.

Then the twelve summoned the multitude of the disciples and said, 'It is not desirable that we should leave the word of God and serve tables. Therefore, brethren, seek out from among you seven men of good reputation, full of the Holy Spirit and wisdom, whom we may appoint over this business; but we will give ourselves continually to prayer and to the ministry of the word' (Acts 6:2-4).

Many times, those in primary leadership in the church are so caught up in management that they do not have time to pray and give clear direction to the work of God. Applying the 'Jethro principle' to the local church would mean that we delegate authority and responsibility to believers who are active in ministry. Unless pastors can release responsibility and authority to the servant leaders at a small group or micro church level, this principle will not work. Micro churches need small groups in their micro church to be most effective. Although elders (or pastors) of the micro church are responsible before the Lord for God's people in the micro church, the small group leaders must be released and trusted with the care of those within their groups.

When Dr. Cho from Seoul, Korea, was at our church in south central Pennsylvania for a pastors' conference, I talked to him about the need to release local leadership in a small group setting. I will never forget his response. "Many pastors are threatened," he said. "They are afraid to release their people." This can also happen in a micro church.

Moses gave Pharaoh the mandate of the Lord: "Let my people go!" God wanted His people to be free to worship Him. I believe that the Lord is likewise setting every believer free from fears or inhibitions that would hold them back from being "able ministers of the new covenant." May every spiritual leader maintain his or her security in the Lord and take the risk of releasing the people of God to minister to others.

When servant leaders release people to minister, the church will grow by leaps and bounds, as it did at the first. But be prepared: with growth comes growing pains. With risk comes both success and failure. Even in the midst of inevitable setbacks, however, be encouraged; making mistakes is part of the process. My wife LaVerne and I have made many mistakes as we have been learning over the past twenty years how to effectively lead healthy micro churches. We have more than forty years of experience with cell groups (small groups) in churches, but only twenty years of leading micro churches. We will give more of our micro church story later in this book.

Training leaders

For effective building of His church, we believe it is God's plan for us to follow Jesus' model of training through small groups. Even if a micro church is only eight or ten persons, there could be a women's small group and a men's small group and a possibly a children's small group within the micro church. The leaders of these smaller groups will go through practical training as they lead the groups and remain accountable to micro church leaders.

Some micro churches encourage prayer partners, where two persons are teamed up to pray for one another for a season between micro church meetings. Other micro churches have used discipleship groups effectively. These discipleship groups may meet during part of the micro church meeting every other week, or they may meet at another time. One micro church we were involved in had a time of eating together, a time of worship, and then an alternating schedule for discipleship groups and larger group meetings. During every other meeting, we met in discipleship groups for about thirty minutes before coming back together at the end of the micro church meeting. The smaller discipleship groups each had a leader. In these groups, we had a time of discussion on a specific passage of scripture followed by a time for praying for each other. It was powerful. People shared things from their lives in these small discipleship meetings of two, three, or four persons that they would never share in a micro church meeting of ten or more. Discipleship group leaders became future micro church leaders. Leading a discipleship group was a part of their leadership training for micro church leadership.

Small groups give everyone an opportunity to get involved. In small groups, each person has the opportunity to fulfill the purpose God has for his or her life. In small groups, people share their lives together and reach out with the healing love of Jesus to a broken world. The small group is a place to receive training, instruction and encouragement while reaching out to friends and neighbors with the Good News of Jesus Christ. With this model, many more leaders are trained to start new micro churches in the future.

Next, we will look at three types of churches that we see around us today.

Notes

1 James Rutz, *The Open Church: How to Bring Back the Exciting Life of the First Century Church,* The SeedSowers (1993), pp 47.
2 T.L. Osborne, *Soul-winning, Out Where the Sinners Are,* (T.L. Osborne Publications, 1967), pp 35-37.

CHAPTER 4

Community Churches, Megachurches, and Micro Churches

The Lord is using many different types of structures to build His church. From the traditional church to the emerging micro church networks, God's Spirit is being poured out on His people. Our God is a God of infinite creativity and variety. We can see this in His creation, from the long-necked graceful giraffe to the multi-colored butterfly. We see His variety in the shades of skin color of His people and the multitude of talents and gifts He gives. God had no interest in producing clones when He created our world.

It is our conviction that God continues to bless variety and creativity in His church through the many different structures and methods He uses to accomplish His purposes. Although I sincerely believe the new micro church networks are tailor-made for today's generation and will be a force in returning us to the New Testament model of church life, I also believe God is using conventional church structures—community churches and megachurches—to play their part in God's future plan. God will build His kingdom regardless of our models, structures or plans.

Those churches that operate within a more traditional setting and those that operate outside of traditional structures are all needed. It is a big job to equip the believers for ministry and bring the gospel to a lost and dying world. We need to employ all the strategies at our disposal to accomplish this task. We need everyone to work together, allowing the new and the old to coexist and complement each other.

We will now look at three necessary types of healthy churches found in the nations today: community churches, megachurches and micro church networks. Their combined strengths will contribute to bringing about God's kingdom here on earth as it is in heaven!

The community church

In nearly every community around the world, you can find what I refer to as "community churches." Most of these churches meet in a church facility each Sunday morning and hold various meetings at the church building throughout the week. There are many styles and flavors of community churches. There is the Methodist flavor, the Baptist flavor, the Congregational flavor, the Episcopal flavor, the Presbyterian flavor, the Vineyard flavor, the Assembly of God flavor, the nondenominational flavor, the independent flavor; the list goes on and on. Some are Calvinistic; some are Arminian. Some are charismatic in their worship expression, while others are more traditional. Some churches are dispensational in their theology, while others focus on the here and now. Some churches are small group-based, and others are not. Some are "seeker-sensitive"—geared for those new to Christianity—while others appeal to the mature Christian. Nearly every Sunday for many years, I have had the privilege of speaking at one of these community churches with their different flavors somewhere in the world. I love the many unique expressions of the body of Christ. It would be boring if each expression looked exactly the same!

My family and I live in rural Lancaster County, Pennsylvania. In this county alone, there are more than six hundred community churches of every kind imaginable. The great majority of these churches have between fifty and two hundred members. Others have four to five hundred or even eight to nine hundred people. When they reach approximately one thousand attendees, if they are in a rural area, they usually fall into another classification—the megachurch—which we will discuss next. Megachurches in metropolitan areas are usually over two thousand persons.

Although community churches range in size, they are all reaching a clear target area: the local populace. In many cases, those who attend and those they reach live in the general geographical area where the community church is located.

Community churches are like community stores

The community church reminds me of a local community store. Where do you buy your groceries? You probably shop at a local grocery store in your community. It might be an independent store, or it could be part of a large chain of stores, but it is the store closest in proximity to where you live. You may personally know the clerks and know where to find specific items on the shelves.

Some neighborhood stores, like community churches, are larger than others, but they still feel like a community store. A community store serves your local area.

Very few people in your neighborhood would drive a long distance to get their groceries. Some even walk to a corner grocery store. Likewise, very few people will drive long distances to worship with other believers who gather each week at their community church facility. Proximity and ease of access are a big part of the very nature of the community church.

More choices

During most of the 20th century, nearly every church in America was a community church (generally a church ranging from fifty to one thousand in attendance). There were very few exceptions. Then something happened. American Christians and American pastors started to hear reports about churches in places like Seoul, Korea, that were massive. When I was a young pastor, we heard that there were over one hundred thousand people in the Yoido Full Gospel Church in Seoul. At the time of this writing, Yoido Full Gospel Church has grown to over eight hundred thousand members.

I remember when Dr. Yonggi Cho, who served as the senior pastor of the world's largest church in Seoul, came to America to explain how pastors in America can also have large churches by "praying and obeying." He taught church leaders to obey the voice of the Holy Spirit and train small group (cell) leaders, then release the ministry of the church to these trained leaders. Through the help of small groups, rapid multiplication and growth occurred.

The megachurch

The new mentality of small groups within the context of large numbers of church members led to a wave of megachurches mushrooming across North America. Many implemented small groups to help them grow. Today, millions of Americans attend megachurches. A megachurch is usually defined as one that has a regular weekly attendance of at least two thousand people. Megachurches are growing rapidly.

Currently, the largest church in North America is Lakewood Church in Houston, Texas with Joel Osteen as its pastor. The average weekly attendance is 43,500. Its denomination is Independent, non-denominational. Unlike most of the megachurches, the Lakewood Church congregation does not meet in various locations. It ranks "number one" in the United States based on the pattern of all members being together in one meeting place.

North Point Community Church was established in November 1995 by Andy Stanley. It is a non-denominational, evangelical Christian megachurch located in Alpharetta, Georgia, a suburb of Atlanta. Today, the church has six campuses, making it the second-largest congregation in the United States.

Life.Church was founded by Craig Groeschel in 1996 with forty members meeting in a two-car garage that was equipped with only a borrowed overhead projector. The membership grew rapidly. Today, it is a multi-church with thirty-two campuses.

Gateway Church is a non-denominational, charismatic Christian multi-site megachurch based in Southlake, Texas, near Dallas. It is the largest congregation in the Dallas-Fort Worth area. Gateway Church is the fourth largest church in North America.

Other megachurches include Saddleback Church in Lake Forest, California with 13 regional campuses, and Dream City Church in Phoenix, Arizona.[1]

A popular Bible teacher and bishop, T. D. Jakes, started his mega-church upon relocating his family and fifty other families from West Virginia, to Dallas, Texas, to establish a new church called "The Pot-ter's House." Within eighteen months, it grew to more than fourteen thousand worshipers! It has been one of the nation's fastest-growing megachurches.[2]

Not only did megachurches like those listed above spring up in major metropolitan areas over the last thirty years or so, they also ap-peared on the rural scene. Today, at least in the United States, it is not unusual for people to drive for an hour or an hour and a half to attend worship services at a megachurch. Megachurches have much to offer. There are ministries for every member of the family, programs for those with addictions, Bible schools, concerts, youth ministries, singles' ministries; you name it, almost anything is available. The megachurch phenomenon has changed the face of the church in North America.

Megachurches are like superstores

I like to call the megachurch the "superstore church." We can look at the example of Walmart, which is a popular superstore chain in the United States. As a young pastor, I had never heard of Walmart since at that time it was a department store chain located mostly in the southern part of our nation. Then it invaded northeastern USA where I live. Now Walmart stores are all over the country! People will drive for an hour or more to shop at a Walmart because they love the low prices, the huge inventory of consumer products and the fact that they can find all they need in one place.

Megachurches, like the Walmart superstores, are large and offer an abundance of services. However, unlike the community church where you may know nearly everyone, at a megachurch you probably know only a few people. Yet, members thoroughly enjoy a megachurch since everything is easily accessible in one location.

In 1980, I started pastoring a church that was meeting in small groups in homes during the week and also in gatherings on Sunday mornings. Using the small group structure, we continued to multiply our numbers until we were in the multi-site megachurch category. Many in this new church drove an hour or more to attend weekly services on Sunday. There was a Bible school, a dynamic youth ministry, a singles' ministry, and a ministry for those who had gone through a divorce. Dozens of short-term mission teams were sent out, and many other specialized ministries were taking place. We met at eight different locations each Sunday and every few months we rented a large auditorium or park where we could meet together as a corporate church. Dr. Cho, the pastor of the world's largest church, came to speak at our church for a leadership conference. Our megachurch had the feel of a spiritual Walmart.

Everyone is different and everyone has different felt needs, so it's not unusual that some people love Walmart while others hardly ever shop there. The same is true when people decide which church to be part of. Some love the megachurch while others feel lost in the crowd and prefer a smaller community church.

Various models of community church and megachurch

Sometimes, larger community churches and megachurches adopt a "mother church" model, whereby many smaller churches relate to the larger, established church. They look to this larger church for oversight, resources and guidance.

At other times the larger community church or megachurch utilizes a multi-site model: one church meeting at various locations. This has become more common due to advances in communication technology. A multi-site church is one local church with one leadership structure that meets physically in several different locations. Each of these models focuses on a larger meeting or on meetings that are held weekly in various locations.

The micro church

As we consider the micro church model, I will draw a comparison with current trends in education. Years ago, I agreed to home school our then sixteen-year-old son, Josh. He had spent eight years in a Christian school and one year in a public school, but he was ready for a change. Initially, when he asked me to consider home schooling him, I thought it would be impossible to do so because of my intense travel schedule. However, as my wife LaVerne and I prayerfully considered the possibility, we felt I should go ahead.

Had I told you fifty years ago I was going to home school our son, you would have looked at me strangely. In fact, you may have thought I was getting involved in some type of new cult. If you recall, fifty years ago, home schooling was almost unheard of in the United States. Nevertheless, early homeschooling advocates made their mark on education and today in North America home schooling is commonplace and well accepted as an alternative to traditional classroom training.

Don't get me wrong. I am not promoting home schooling as the pinnacle of educational experience. I am using this as an example, in the sense that parents today have the choice of home school along with the more traditional choices of public or private schooling. All three types of educational models coexist in nearly every community in North America.

In a way that is similar to the home school phenomenon, micro church networks are also mushrooming all across parts of the world. Like our educational choices, they will coexist and network with other more traditional community churches and megachurches in our communities. God will use and bless all three forms of church—the community churches, the megachurches, and the micro church networks.

We can draw an analogy between micro church networks and the stores in a shopping mall. If the average store found in a shopping mall was taken out of the mall to stand on its own, it would die within a year. The normal store in a shopping mall needs the others to survive. Each specialized store flourishes together within the cluster of the others. Yet each one is fully a store in its own right, despite being in a mall.

Micro churches could be compared to these shopping mall stores. They are individual and specialized, yet they seem to flourish when they network together with other micro churches. We will explain later how they network, but for now, let's look at how each one functions as a real church, and how the micro church model compares to the community church and megachurch models.

Micro churches have a unique mentality

The concept of micro church requires a different way of thinking about church than we have been used to. Believers in micro churches do not focus on growing larger in the same way that those in a community church or megachurch would. Their focus is on growth through multiplication, or through starting new micro churches. One way of thinking is not right and the other wrong; they are just different. Think of the Christian school, the public school and the home school. Which model is correct? Actually, they are all correct, depending on which approach you believe the Lord wants you to take.

Micro churches are small. Therefore, they can meet anywhere—in a house, in a college dorm room, in a coffee shop, under a tree, or in a corporate boardroom. They meet in these locations and do not think of growing to a size that would require the construction of a building to accommodate a larger group. Instead, they ask, "How can we multiply leaders and start more micro churches?" "How can we walk together as micro church leaders?" And although some micro churches meet on Sundays, many others meet at other times during the week. Micro churches are simple and flexible.

The Lord is doing the same thing all over the world

About ten years after planting a new church in the early 1980s, we received a phone call from Ralph Neighbour's office. I knew from his book, *Where Do We Go from Here?* that the Lord had used Ralph to open the hearts of thousands worldwide to the cell group movement. Since he was scheduled to speak in New Jersey, our neighboring state, he asked to meet with me. I drove with our office administrator to New Jersey and met with Ralph during a break in his speaking engagement.

"Tell me your story," Ralph said. As I told him about our church starting with one small group and growing to over 2,300 people all participating in small groups, tears began to stream down his face. "The Lord is doing the same thing all over the world," Ralph exclaimed. "People who have never met, have never heard of one another, are using the same terminology because the Lord is doing the same thing through them in many parts of the world. This is truly the Lord."

As I travel week after week, I find the same being said of micro church networks. The Lord is doing the same thing through them in many parts of the world. They are springing up in many nations. They are using similar terminology and methods, in spite of the fact that they have never met one another. This is truly the hand of God.

Complementary expressions of the body of Christ

Like any church, micro churches can get off-track. Not every micro church will be a perfect example of a community of people in close-knit, interpersonal relationships with a common mission. Relational Christianity in micro churches can be messy.

If you have been turned off by those involved in micro churches who have been exclusive, bitter, or proud, please do not "throw the baby out with the bath water," so to speak. A group should be forewarned that when they take on a mentality that their group is best ("Us four, no more!"), they are on dangerous ground. We must guard against a mentality of micro church vs. organized church or 'us' vs. 'them.'

I have prayed with believers from micro churches who have been hurt by believers from community churches and megachurches. However, I have also prayed with leaders and believers from community churches and megachurches who have been offended by the pride and arrogance of believers involved in micro churches. If any kind of church (community, mega or micro) becomes controlling or exclusive in its thinking, it has derailed. We are all a part of the worldwide body of Christ. There is only one church, and we must make every effort to walk in unity. Love always believes the best (1 Corinthians 13:5-6). The Lord will take us in our weakness and bring good out of us if we submit to Him.

Since all of these are expressions of the body of Christ, the question remains: which type of church has the Lord called you to be involved in? Much of this comes down to personal preference. I drive a Ford Escape. But the Ford Motor Company sells many other models including the Ford Focus and the Ford Mustang. All of these models are Ford vehicles.

Which model of church is most biblical?

You may wonder which of the three models of church is best: the community church, the megachurch, or the micro church network. The answer is, all three are! It just depends on which one you are called to. God will use whichever structure He chooses, and He does not necessarily ask for our opinions about how to go about extending His kingdom.

A few years ago, I was so encouraged while sitting with believers in a traditional Anglican church building, Holy Trinity Brompton, in London, England, where believers were experiencing a powerful move of God. The Lord has used these believers to make the Alpha Course available to literally millions of people around the globe.

As soon as we think our group is the only "right" group around town, we get in trouble. Pride always comes before a fall. We must, with great conviction, follow the path the Lord has laid out for us, and at the same time, honor what He is doing through others who are doing it differently than we are.

If you do not have a personal call from God to plant a micro church but desire to be a part of a micro church, ask God to help you find someone who has a call to plant a new church, or find a micro church already operating. Partner with them by praying, by helping them financially and by encouraging them. The person you partner with might be in your local area, somewhere in your nation or perhaps in another part of the world. Develop a partnership with them and receive the blessing from the Lord as they plant new micro churches. Remember, Jesus said that when we give a prophet a cup of cold water in His name, we will receive a reward like theirs (Matthew 10:41, 42).

God has many models for His church, and different believers have different preferences. Let's be secure in the church model we prefer, and honor others who have different preferences. As we serve in the places and ways God has called us to, His Kingdom will expand for His glory.

Notes

1   Margaret Minnicks, "The Largest Churches in America and How They Grew so Quickly," https://owlcation.com/humanities

2   Jim Jones, "Swift Growth Shapes Potter's House," www.christianitytoday.com, January 12, 1998

CHAPTER 5

Our Story: Community Church to Megachurch to the New Micro Churches

People are the church. Churches of all kinds spring up and flourish when people allow the Lord to use them for His purposes. Allow me to share with you the roots of our church as it evolved from being a community church, growing to a megachurch, and then to starting new micro church networks.

As I mentioned earlier, my wife LaVerne and I led a small group of dedicated believers to start a small group-based church in our community. This was due to an increasing need for a new wineskin to accommodate the new wine (new believers). It all started during the summer of 1971 when my future wife, LaVerne, and I helped start a youth ministry with a small band of young people who were reaching out to the unchurched youth of our community in northern Lancaster County, Pennsylvania. We played sports and conducted various activities throughout the week for spiritually-needy youngsters and teenagers. This kind of friendship evangelism produced results. During the next few years, dozens of young people came to faith in Christ with a desire to find their place in a local church.

Every Sunday night we took vanloads of these new believers to various churches in our community because we wanted to help them get involved in a local church. After the church services, the entire group usually returned to our home for a time of praise, prayer, spiritual counseling and just plain fun. Our desire was to teach and model what practical Christian living was all about.

Those of us who served in this youth ministry were from various local churches, so we sincerely wanted to help the new believers find their place in our local congregations. We quickly discovered that although Christians in the local churches were friendly and helpful, these new believers were not getting connected. The young believers simply were not being assimilated into the life of the established churches.

The need for flexible wineskins

The answer to the dilemma came when a church leader shared from Matthew 9:16-17 concerning new wine and wineskins. The "new wineskin" is a new model of church structure, tailored to serve and equip new believers in Jesus Christ, who can be likened to the "new wine."

A wineskin is like a balloon. It needs to be flexible and pliable. Putting new Christians into old structures can cause the structures to break and the new Christians may be lost. New Christians should be placed in new structures which are flexible and capable of encouraging spiritual growth.

It was clear there was a need for a New Testament church flexible enough to relate to believers from all kinds of backgrounds. So, in October 1980, a group of approximately twenty-five believers met for the first time for a Sunday morning celebration in a living room. "DOVE Christian Fellowship" had officially begun. There was an atmosphere of excitement among us as we also met in three separate home groups during the week. The focus was not on Sunday morning meetings. The focus was on the church meeting from house to house.

During the next ten years, the church grew to over 2,300 believers scattered throughout communities in a seven-county area of Pennsylvania. We had now reached the megachurch classification. These believers met in more than 125 small groups during the week. On Sunday mornings, clusters of small groups came together in five different locations. We had become a multi-site church. The whole church came together several times each year on a Sunday morning in a large gymnasium or at a local park amphitheater for a corporate service.

Whenever a congregation's Sunday morning celebration outgrew its rented facility, they either moved to a larger facility or began two or three new celebrations meeting in the same building. Our goal was to multiply the small groups and celebrations by beginning new celebrations and new small groups in other areas as God gave the increase. We also found that by renting buildings at an economical rate, we had more money available to use for world missions. During these years, churches were planted in Scotland, Brazil, Kenya and New Zealand. These overseas churches followed the same house-to-house principles as those we were using in North America.

We decided to give our church away

As DOVE International grew, it became clear that in order for us to accomplish the vision God had given us, we would have to make major adjustments. If we wanted to build the church with a focus on discipleship through small groups in the nations of the world, we would have to give the church away. When a father gives his daughter to her husband-to-be on her wedding day, he realizes he has invested many years in training his daughter for this very moment—to give her away.

That is exactly what we did with the church. Giving the church away better suited our vision of a small group-based church planting movement intent on training a new generation of church planters and leaders. The DOVE church in south central Pennsylvania became eight individual churches, each with its own eldership team. We formed an Apostolic Council to give oversight to all the churches of DOVE. Then we gave each of the eight celebrations the freedom to become autonomous—they had the option of joining with the DOVE family of churches or connecting to another part of the body of Christ. Each of these eight churches affirmed their desire to be part of the DOVE family of churches. Churches that we had helped to plant in Kenya, Uganda, and New Zealand also confirmed their desire to partner with this new international family of churches.

This time of change was not easy for us. I enjoyed being the senior pastor of a megachurch along with the security it brought. Those of us on the leadership team and staff of DOVE had to walk in a new level of faith for finances. The finances we had received each week from the tithes of one megachurch were now given to each autonomous small group-based church. Of course, obedience always pays off. In the years since the transition, the Lord has always faithfully provided!

DOVE's family of small group-based churches collaborating together continues to grow. We are currently a network of over one thousand churches and many ministries across six continents. Our family of churches today includes community churches, churches on a path to becoming megachurches, and micro church networks.

It's time to "pray and obey" again

When I think of the beginnings of our new church plant in 1980, I realize it actually started as a micro church. It had all the components of a little church by itself with leadership developed in-house. When we made the move to a larger building after outgrowing the living room, the dynamics changed considerably. We needed to develop the "temple ministry" of church life as we met for a larger celebration on a Sunday morning in addition to our small groups. The evolution of this change resulted in a more traditional community church much like the other churches in our area, despite our unique small group-based structure.

Time marches on. What was new and unique several years ago soon becomes an old wineskin.

I believe it is time again to pray and obey. Many believers are dreaming of another type of church in North America—the micro church network. I am so grateful to those who prepared the way for me, as a young man, to start a unique wineskin that was different from the status quo.

A new day has arrived, again. The Lord has been instructing me and many of my generation to prepare the way for the next generation of church planters and church leaders who will model a new type of church for the next generation. I am excited about the feasibility of micro churches opening even more possibilities for discipleship of the nations.

In today's church world, you can find local community churches and the superstore megachurches everywhere. The Lord has and will continue to use both. However, He will also use micro church networks with their simplistic approaches and structures to build His kingdom. Let's open our hearts to this revolutionary force that is growing quietly in humble micro churches across the nation and around the world. We need to "keep all options open" so the Lord can use all His servants to function together as one body to change the world.

CHAPTER 6

The Growth of
Micro Churches Globally

In this chapter, we will look at the growth of major micro church movements in the world today.

China's micro church movement

The revival in China today is considered the largest spiritual harvest since the book of Acts. The Chinese Cultural Revolution with its severe persecution of Christians did not suppress the church as it intended to do. Instead, it fueled the revival. Today, an estimated twenty-five thousand Chinese are becoming Christians every day through various micro church movements that have sprung up throughout their nation. There are over eighty million believers in these unregistered micro churches in China.

An article in *The Atlantic* puts it this way:

China, the world's rising superpower, is experiencing an explosion of faith. The decades of anti-religious campaigns that followed the 1949 communist takeover are giving way to a spiritual transformation—and among the fastest-growing drivers of that transformation are unregistered churches. Once called "house" or "underground" churches because they were small clandestine affairs, these groups have become surprisingly well-organized, meeting very openly and often counting hundreds of congregants. They've helped the number of Protestants soar from about 1 million when the communists took power to at least 60 million today. Of these believers, about two-thirds are not affiliated with government churches. In other words, Protestants in non-government churches outnumber worshippers in government churches two to one.[1]

On two occasions I have had the opportunity to minister to leaders of underground church movements in China. Both times were life-changing for me. Meeting these humble men and women of God deeply moved me. I know one thing for sure: they taught me far more than I could teach them.

During one gathering, ninety-five percent of the leaders in attendance had been imprisoned for their faith. Many of them had traveled four days by train to get to the secluded venue for the seminar. One elderly leader had just been released from prison four days before. One precious man of God, who sat at our breakfast table, told us humbly that he gives leadership to ten million believers meeting in micro churches in the micro church network he oversees. The Chinese leaders call these small micro churches house churches. I sat and listened in amazement! It was as if I were in another world.

I also met a group of women who oversee house church leaders, one of whom was responsible for four hundred thousand believers involved in a house church network. They told stories of being raped in prison, yet they have stayed true to the Lord and continue to birth house churches as people are coming to Christ all over their nation.

I was asked to teach about becoming spiritual fathers and mothers. After many of the sessions, these precious men and women of God stood, prayed and repented. It was such a humbling experience. They repented because they felt they were so caught up in the work of God that they were not focusing enough on the workers of God. This is a great lesson for all of us. We can become so caught up in God's work, including the starting of new micro churches, that we lose sight of our call from the Lord to be a spiritual father or mother to the next generation.

The Chinese church has gone "underground" in house churches out of necessity. But they are committed to following this biblical pattern, regardless of any changes that might take place in their national or political regulations. If they were to register their churches in the current system, they would not be permitted to teach their children about Christ in church settings until they were eighteen years of age. This is not an option for them.

When I asked the Chinese leaders if the people in their house churches tithe, they said "yes." When I asked them if the house church pastors receive support from the tithe, they smiled and informed me that only those individuals who are willing to be sent out as missionaries or apostolic leaders to other parts of China receive any financial support. This is also true of most house church leaders in North America. They either have a business or work at a job to support themselves and their families. They are "tent-makers" like Aquila and Priscilla who had a church in their home (Romans 16:3-5; 1 Corinthians 16:19). Only when they have the responsibility to oversee other house church leaders are leaders supported financially.

God is pouring out His grace on the Chinese church. This "underground church" is probably experiencing the greatest move of God in history since Pentecost. I feel that the underground church in China is the most strategically organized church in the world. Their rapid growth is happening in and through house churches.

On both of my trips to China, I came home forever changed. May we all learn from their humility and desperation for God.

Persecution on the rise

Open Doors, founded by Brother Andrew in 1955, continues to stand with the persecuted church until today. The organization aims to raise awareness of global persecution and mobilize prayer, support and action among Christians from around the world.

The focus on China taken from the "watch list" of Open Doors explains:

> The management of religious affairs in China lies with the Communist Party now, not just with the government. And Christians are intensely and increasingly feeling this shift and fear of Christian persecution. Since the Communist Party took over, the implementation of the regulations on religion, the treatment of religious groups, especially Christians, be-

came much harsher across the country. Crackdowns against Christians happen countrywide, both in state-approved and non-registered churches. The youth are increasingly being removed from church life; worship is monitored via CCTV and spies; teachers and medical workers are told they are not allowed to have any religious affiliation…. New restrictions on the internet, social media and NGOs—and the new regulations on religion—are all seriously limiting freedom.

Fifteen days before Christmas 2018, one of China's largest house churches in Chengdu was raided by Chinese police. The raid continued for days, resulting in arrests and detainments of more than 100 Christians, including Early Rain Covenant Church pastor Wang Yi. He is one of China's most well-known pastors. A week later, another large underground congregation, the Rongguili Church, was closed by local authorities.[2]

Learning from the China situation

It might be religious persecution, political intrigue, restrictions such as those we experienced during the coronavirus pandemic of 2020, or any other barriers that prevent the church from meeting openly or in large numbers. Any one of these factors has the potential to single-handedly limit the basic functions of traditional church meetings. Of course, it is possible for a megachurch or community church to hold online services, meet on social media platforms and distribute teachings through the internet when faced with certain restrictions. But the core component of coming together, openly and in large numbers, could easily be halted.

Most of these barriers, however, would not affect the micro church as harshly. Thus, the term "underground." Micro churches that meet covertly in small gatherings and homes are much more protected from external interference. The situation in China, the chronicles of the early church as reported in the book of Acts, and testimonies from many other nations experiencing religious persecution demonstrate this. "When the enemy shall come in like a flood, the Spirit of the LORD shall lift up a standard against him" (Isaiah 59:19b).

As I write, coronavirus is raging throughout the nations. In many places, churches are not permitted to meet at all. In other places, meetings are restricted to a maximum of five to fifteen persons. I believe that by God's grace, the church of Christ will emerge even stronger through this pandemic.

Stephen Strang, founder of Charisma Magazine, explains how God is moving in mighty ways even during the COVID-19 outbreak in China.

I recently had an eye-opening interview with Pastor Frank Amedia, whose ministry, POTUS Shield, has a close alliance with the Christian community in China. "We've had reports of Christians being healed of this virus by the power of God and the healing of God," he says. "My sources tell me the same thing, whenever there is this kind of a problem—like there was with SARS." Amedia says the coronavirus is the third plague to hit China in the span of this generation. He points out that when the people can't rely on their government, they look for help elsewhere—and that's when the church has the opportunity to shine brightly with the gospel.

"We're being told that people are coming in swarms to churches, house churches, that there's gospel and evangelism going out in the streets, person to person, that there's supernatural healing."[3]

The plagues and persecutions this world faces need not squelch the church of Jesus Christ. It is our prayer that as the church is willing to create new wineskins to overcome any earthly challenges, people will keep coming to Jesus and revival will sweep the nations. I believe micro churches are one of these new wineskins God is using to build His church in the midst of current world events.

In restricted areas, churches can meet in homes

Restrictions are not new to the church of Christ. In many cities, zoning restrictions prohibit the building of church buildings within city limits. This puts a lot of limitations on traditional church models, especially among exploding urban populations. Micro churches are an obvious solution to this dilemma; believers can meet in homes!

In some parts of the world, micro churches start as a matter of necessity due to various restrictions or legal bans. In the book *House to House,*[4] I tell the story of a church in Ethiopia that was forced "underground." In 1982, half of the evangelical churches in Ethiopia were closed due to harassment, legal banning, and persecution. The Meserete Kristos Church was completely banned. All their church buildings were seized and used for other purposes. Several of their prominent leaders were imprisoned for years without trial or charges.

The church membership at that time was approximately five thousand. As the fires of persecution grew hotter and hotter each year, they were forced to go underground and meet in clandestine home groups. Nearly a decade later the Marxist government fell. The same government leaders who closed the doors of the church buildings a few years earlier led the procession of God's people back into the buildings. However, the most startling news was that the church had grown, while "underground," from five thousand to over fifty thousand people!

During persecution, these believers met from house to house in small groups. Hundreds of believers began to get involved in the work of ministry in these small micro churches. They no longer were focusing on the church building or the programs of the church. Their time together was spent in prayer, reaching the lost, and making disciples.

God's agenda for the building of His kingdom includes two elements: laborers and harvest. He wants laborers trained to bring in the full harvest. "My food," said Jesus, "is to do the will of him who sent me and to finish his work. Do you not say, 'Four months more and then the harvest'? I tell you, open your eyes and look at the fields! They are ripe for harvest" (John 4:34-36).

The Baptists initiate church planting movements

Yet another example of church expansion in times of crisis is seen in several church planting movements initiated by the Southern Baptist Mission Board. In the late 1980's, the Southern Baptist Mission Board made a paradigm shift in their approach to missions. They decided to plant churches by training and releasing as it was done in the book of Acts. They developed a Church Planting Movement (CPM) strategy and defined a church planting movement as a rapid and exponential increase of indigenous churches planting churches within a given people group or population segment. The strategy was implemented as church planters became spiritual fathers and mothers who trained and released their spiritual sons and daughters to become new micro church planters.

In the decade that followed, church growth was indeed rapid and exponential. One factor that fueled the growth of these micro church networks in Latin America was the severe economic crisis in the early 1990s. Church members were prevented from traveling long distances to their church buildings so they "moved their meetings into homes and found that growth greatly accelerated."[5] In one Latin American area, 129 churches increased to 1,918 churches in just nine years.

In India, they started with twenty-eight churches in 1989 that grew to two thousand churches in less than ten years. These results have been duplicated in Cambodia, a country with an infrastructure in shambles due to wars and dictatorships. In the same time period, they grew from six to 194 churches. A majority of these churches are networked micro churches.

In India, the Baptists implemented a plan to send out disciples two by two just as Jesus did in Luke chapter 10. They found "men of peace" in targeted villages, moved in with them and began discipling their families. "As these initial converts came to faith, they led their families to the Lord, baptized them and forged them into the nucleus of new churches in each village."[6]

As the Baptist church planting movement unfolded in Cambodia, the momentum burned from within. "Local leaders expressed their own vision for planting churches in every district and within each ethnic community. As they acquired training and encouragement, the primary church planters were the church members themselves, rather than missionaries or professional church planters. The coordinator later observed that 'churches planted by other churches are reproducible, but those started by funded church planters are not (with few exceptions)."[7]

Key factors for church planting movement success

The Baptists claim there are several key components to Church Planting Movements (CPMs). First, they reproduce rapidly. Second, there is a multiplicative increase. This type of increase is only possible when new churches are being started by the churches themselves—rather than by professional church planters or missionaries. Third, they are indigenous churches. This means they are generated from within rather than from without. The gospel nearly always enters a people group from the outside; this is the task of the missionary. This is not to say that the gospel is not able to spring up intuitively within a people group. However, in a church planting movement, the momentum put in motion by missionaries quickly becomes indigenous, such that the initiative and drive of the movement comes from within the people group rather than from those outside.

One of the key elements of these CPMs is house churches. The Baptists explain, "The vast majority of the churches continue to be small, reproducible cell churches of ten to thirty members meeting in homes or storefronts."[8]

What about church planting movements in the west?

The successful CPMs of the Baptist church are in largely non-western cultures. Here below, author of Church Planting Movements, David Garrison, speaks out about why he believes we have not seen huge movements in the western world yet:

> One of the common characteristics that we've seen of church planting movements is persecution, and in many open democracies, you don't have that. Persecution often creates a climate of urgent need in response to Christ. This is one of the factors noted in why we don't see more CPM's in the West. One CPM that we did see was in Amsterdam among immigrants, refugees who came into the area. They were extremely responsive and began reproducing churches at a rapid clip.

> There is an awful lot to commend house churches in the United States. There are quantifiable realities, such as the cost

of church buildings, the exploding population, the increase in urbanization and the increasing cost of property in the cities. There is no way we can build enough church buildings. It becomes a question of stewardship. Can you justify putting 20-30 million dollars into building a church just so that you can add another 1,000 people to a church that already has a couple of thousand people? When we understand that people make up the church rather than church buildings, more and more people will come to the conclusion that we have to have new wineskins for the body of Christ.

I am concerned about the 80+ million unchurched Americans. I'm not convinced that our existing structures will draw them in. The house church movement has the potential to do that. It does not yet appear as it shall be. We are still in a transition stage. I'm excited to see what the models are that will emerge from this.[9]

I agree with Garrison's assessment of why church planting movements are so important, and why they are not growing as rapidly in our western culture as they are in the developing world. But it does not need to stay that way. It is in our best interests in North America to think in terms of starting CPMs, not just local micro churches. If you have a vision from the Lord to plant a micro church, go to your knees until you receive a clear vision to start or help start a CPM. When Barnabas and Saul were sent out of the church in Antioch in Acts 13, they started a church planting movement. Acts 13, 14 and 15 tell the story of this new CPM that emerged from house to house nearly everywhere they went.

We need a spiritual rabbit plague

Wolfgang Simson says we need a "spiritual rabbit plague." I'm sure you know that elephants and rabbits have vastly different gestation periods and fertility capabilities. Rabbits multiply quickly while elephants produce their young less often. Both a rapid rabbit proliferation and slower elephant proliferation are needed to carry the gospel to all the earth.

I believe the rapid rabbit-kind of reproduction will happen through the third kind of church, micro church networks. Because the micro church model lends itself to quick reproduction of leaders, the numerical potential of micro church networks is enormous. Simson writes:

> As we all work together towards discipling the nations and filling the earth with the knowledge of the Lord like water covers the sea, we should all appreciate and acknowledge elephant-type structures and churches. God has blessed through them, is using them and will continue to use them. However, I am convinced that the bulk of the work of discipling whole nations is calling loud and clear for something beyond that, which I call a spiritual rabbit plague.

ELEPHANTS	RABBITS
fertile four times a year	practically continuously fertile
one baby per pregnancy	average of seven babies per pregnancy
22-month gestation period	1-month gestation period
sexual maturity: 18 years	sexual maturity: 4 months
grow in 3 years from 2 to 3	grow in 3 years from 2 to 476 million

With several million churches still needed to fill the earth, it's going to take both elephants and rabbits to get the job done![10]

Cell groups have opened the door for micro churches

I have had the privilege of being involved in churches based on a small group structure for over forty years. In fact, this is the only type of church structure to which I have personally given leadership. Today, churches of nearly all denominations are receiving a revelation from the Lord that the believers should be the ministers. So, I get the opportunity to train leaders in effective small group ministry throughout the nations.

Because of this, I am convinced that the most effective micro church networks will be made up of small group-based micro churches. Obviously, when a new micro church begins, it starts as one small group. But as it grows, wise micro church leaders will train leaders within the group to lead small satellite groups as part of their leadership training for future micro church leadership. One micro church could be comprised of several small groups. These small groups could meet for a portion of the micro church meeting in separate rooms of the house. Or, in addition to the micro church meeting each week, smaller groups of believers could also meet for breakfast or at another time to pray together and be accountable with their Christian lives.

The small group-based movement has been used by the Lord to open up the church at large to the truths of the priesthood of every believer. It has also opened the door for healthy micro church networks to emerge. Many small group-based churches will birth micro churches in the coming years. I meet pastors of community churches and megachurches who are now focusing on releasing new micro churches from their church with a vision to start a micro church network. The leadership of the micro church will continue to look to the senior pastor and the elders of the sending church for oversight as they enter this holy experiment.

When I was in England training Anglican vicars in small group-based ministry, I could see that the Lord is doing some amazing things within the organized church of England. Many are realizing that people learn by doing, and a most effective way to learn to minister is through small groups. But even with this new expression of church life, many are searching for something beyond current church experience. When I shared with them about micro church networks, they seemed to come alive with fresh vision for the future.

Notes

1 Ian Johnson, "In China, Unregistered Churches are Driving a Religious Revolution," www.theatlantic.com/international/archive, April 23, 2017

2 Open Doors USA, www.opendoorsusa.org/christian-persecution/world-watch-list/china

3   Stephen Strang, The Strang Report (Reuters) https://www.charismamag.com/blogs/the-strang-report/44382-reports-of-supernatural-healing-revivals-in-midst-of-coronavirus-outbreak

4   Larry Kreider, *House to House*, (Ephrata, PA: House to House Publications, 1995)

5   David Garrison, *Church Planting Movements*, (Richmond, VA: International Mission Board of the Southern6Baptist Convention, 1999) p. 14

6   Ibid., p. 23

7   Ibid., p. 30

8   Ibid., p. 35

9   House2House Magazine, "A Telephone Interview with David Garrison," Issue 2, p. 9

10 Wolfgang Simson, *Houses that Change the World*, (Cumbria, UK: OM Publishing, 2001), p. 106

CHAPTER 7

The Role of Spiritual Fathers and Mothers: Make Disciples

A major aspect of micro church ministry is preparing and training present and future spiritual fathers and mothers and then releasing them to reproduce themselves. Paul, the apostle, told the Corinthian church that they desperately needed fathers. "Even though you have ten thousand guardians in Christ, you do not have many fathers; for in Christ Jesus I became your father through the gospel. Therefore, I urge you to imitate me" (1 Corinthians 4:15-16).

Unless we become spiritual fathers and mothers, we are in danger of losing the next generation. The Bible displays a family perspective that can help us understand spiritual families and spiritual parenting in His body. God is identified as the God of Abraham, Isaac and Jacob in the Old Testament. His very name acknowledges continuity through several generations.

In the New Testament, Paul, the apostle, spoke of four generations when he called Timothy his son and exhorted him to find faithful men to whom he could impart what Paul taught him: "And the things you [second generation] have heard me [first generation] say in the presence of many witnesses, entrust to reliable men [third generation] who will also be qualified to teach others [fourth generation]" (2 Timothy 2:2). Paul was thinking about his spiritual posterity and speaking as a spiritual father to his spiritual son Timothy.

The Lord wants to see spiritual families continually reproducing in each generation. He has a generational perspective, and we must have that perspective as well. Micro churches are an ideal wineskin in which spiritual fathers and mothers can train the next generation to become spiritual fathers and mothers. If we understand how a healthy natural family functions, we will understand how a healthy spiritual family should function.

I will never forget the experience of having our first baby. I had faithfully attended prenatal classes with LaVerne where I learned how to coach her through pains leading up the childbirth. But when the contractions started, this was new territory. I had never done this before. I felt to tell LaVerne, "Couldn't you just put it on hold for a few months?" But waiting was not an option. She was going to give birth, and our baby girl was to be born now—whether I felt ready or not.

It felt rather strange being a "papa." We had never been down this road before. Somehow, with the faithful advice of trusted family and friends, it all worked out.

When this "baby" girl got married, we gave her away. She had gone from being a baby, to a teenager, to an adult. Now, she was ready to go and parent the next generation. Our daughter has gone on to give birth to three children of her own. These grandchildren of ours will likely be parents themselves one day, and another generation will be born!

When it comes to spiritual parenting, many potential spiritual parents go through similar emotions and fears. "How could God ever use me to be a spiritual parent? What if I can't do it properly? Am I really ready for this?" However, as they are encouraged to take steps of faith and obedience, they begin to experience the joy of becoming a spiritual father or mother. They have the satisfaction of training and releasing others for eternity.

Only a dysfunctional parent will try to hang on to his or her children and use them to fulfill the parent's own vision. Healthy parents expect their children to leave their home to start their own families. Healthy spiritual parents must think the same way. This generation of Christian leaders are called to "give away" many of the believers in their churches to start their own spiritual families—in many cases new micro churches.

According to the Bible, there are three different types of people in our churches: spiritual children, young men, and fathers. 1 John

2:12-13 tells us, "I write to you, dear children, because your sins have been forgiven on account of his name. I write to you, fathers, because you have known him who is from the beginning. I write to you, young men, because you have overcome the evil one..." Let's look at these three types of people and how they can be prepared and trained to become spiritual parents.

1. Spiritual children

There are many spiritual babies (new Christians) in the church today, with few spiritual fathers and mothers available to disciple them. Nevertheless, the larger problem seems to be the many "spiritual baby Christians" who never grew up—many of whom are unaware they are still spiritual infants. Their spiritual chronological age may be twenty, thirty, forty or fifty years, but they remain on "milk." They make a fuss when they don't get their own way, complain about not being fed, and have not yet taken spiritual responsibility to train the next generation.

2. Spiritual young men and women

Spiritual young men (and women), according to the Bible, have the Word of God abiding in them and have overcome the wicked one. They have learned to feed on the Word for themselves in order to overcome the devil, but they have not yet become spiritual fathers or mothers.

When I was a child, I thought my father knew everything. When I became an adolescent, I noticed there were a few things he didn't know. By the time I was in my mid-teens, in my youthful arrogance I just figured my father was still living in the stone ages. It seemed to me that he understood almost nothing. However, when I became a father, I was amazed at how much my father had learned over the past few years! The truth is, when I became a father, my perspective changed. I was able to appreciate my father's wisdom in ways I had not recognized before. In the same way, having spiritual children also changes our perspective.

3. Spiritual fathers and mothers

One of the greatest catalysts to maturity as a Christian is to become a spiritual father or mother. Many of the problems that surface in churches today are caused by spiritual young men and women who are full of the Word of God but have not had the experience of becoming spiritual parents. Another cause of problems is the situation of church leaders not releasing spiritual young men and women within their churches to have their own spiritual children. Micro churches solve these training and leadership issues because they develop spiritual fathers and mothers in-house in a natural, family-like setting.

Birthing a spiritual lineage

In Genesis 15:1, when God spoke to Abraham about a promised spiritual seed, He said, "Do not be afraid, Abram. I am your shield, your very great reward." When God gives us a spiritual revelation to be spiritual parents, we need not be afraid. We may make mistakes or sometimes get hurt by people we are helping, but we have a shield to protect us. God will be our great reward.

Abraham was ninety-nine years old when God gave him the promise that he would be the "father of many nations" (Genesis 17:4). One of the covenant promises was that his descendants would be "as numerous as the stars in the sky" (Genesis 26:4).

Although this covenant is speaking about the covenant between God and Abraham and the Jewish people, Galatians 3:29 says that those who belong to Christ are "Abraham's seed, and heirs according to the promise." Therefore, as believers, God wants to birth "nations" from us, also. These "nations" or groups of people who come to know God because of our influence will be our spiritual lineage—they are our posterity in God's kingdom. We have been promised it because we are children of promise. Our God desires to give us a spiritual posterity.

A spiritual parent defined

Before we can be effective spiritual fathers or mothers and see our posterity emerge, we must first check our motives. Spiritual parenting is a "behind the scenes" task. Probably no one will pat us on the back and say, "What a good job you are doing: keep up the good work." Why? Because being a father or mother is not something we do, as much as it is something we are. I do not have to tell people that I am a father. They know it when they see my son and daughters.

Scripture warns us about giving ourselves an impressive title in an effort to gain the honor and respect of others: "Do not call anyone on earth your father; for One is your Father, He who is in heaven...but he who is greatest among you shall be your servant" (Matthew 23:9,11). A spiritual father or mother is not a title or position. It is a role of servanthood. A spiritual parent who is a small group leader or a micro church leader is always a servant first. No one can ever take the place of our heavenly Father. Spiritual fathers and mothers point their spiritual children to their heavenly Father.

Paul, the apostle, called himself a father several times in scripture, but he uses the word "father" to denote "not authority, but affection: therefore he calls them not his obliged, but his beloved, sons" (see 1 Corinthians 4:14).[1] The measure of greatness of a spiritual parent is one's level of servanthood and love, not one's position.

Spiritual fathers and mothers could also be called mentors. The term mentor comes from a story in Greek mythology in which Odysseus asked his friend, Mentor, to look after his son while he went on a long journey. A spiritual mentor recognizes that people need to be developed through a caring and empathetic approach.

My favorite definition of a spiritual parent is this: A spiritual father or mother helps a spiritual son or daughter reach his or her God-given potential. It is that uncomplicated and yet profound. Bobb Biehl says it this way: "Mentoring is more about 'how can I help you?' than 'what should I teach you?'"[2]

More than forty-five years ago, LaVerne and I and a team of young people began to develop Paul-Timothy relationships with new Christians. I would meet with a few young men each week for Bible study and prayer and would try to answer their questions about life. LaVerne did the same with young women. Watching them grow from spiritual babies to young men and women to spiritual parents has brought us great joy. It has also produced growth in our own spiritual lives.

How do we become spiritual fathers or mothers?

So how does a young man or woman become a spiritual parent? The only way is to have children—then be committed to helping them grow. This happens either by spiritual adoption (becoming a spiritual father or mother to someone who is already a believer but needs to be discipled) or by spiritual natural birth (becoming a spiritual father or mother to someone you have personally led to Christ). Paul became a spiritual father to Onesimus through "natural birth," leading him to Christ when he was in prison (Philemon 10). Paul became a spiritual father to Timothy through "adoption" after meeting him in Ephesus (Acts 16:1-4).

The micro church and small group provide ideal opportunities for everyone to experience a spiritual family and eventually become spiritual parents themselves. When micro churches and small groups multiply, new spiritual parents have the opportunity to take responsibility and start a new spiritual family (micro church or small group) themselves.

A sweeping revival is just around the corner. God's people need to be alert to accommodate the great harvest this will bring into the kingdom of God. Spiritual parents will need to be ready to obey His call and take these young Christians under their wings. God has called us to be spiritual parents. The Lord wants to give us a spiritual legacy. We may not feel ready; in fact, we may feel unprepared. Nevertheless, God's call remains on our lives.

Healthy families will multiply

Multiplication is a fact of nature. Our God is a God of multiplication, and He wants us to also be fruitful and multiply (Genesis 1:28).

As a farm boy, I once counted the kernels on a healthy stalk of corn and found something close to 1,200 kernels. This would be the second generation, having come from just one seed. Do you know that at the same rate of multiplication, there could be one million, four hundred forty thousand kernels of corn by the third generation? That is quite impressive!

In the same way, healthy cells in the body multiply and result in growth. A living cell is in a state of constant activity.

The church in the book of Acts multiplied rapidly because they understood the value of believers meeting in homes in spiritual family relationships. They functioned in close relationship with each other. This activity and interdependence resulted in healthy growth for the early church.

As the Lord restores spiritual family life into His kingdom today, the church in our generation will also multiply rapidly. We must be ready. We must properly train and prepare spiritual parents, sons and daughters, so that Christ may be formed in them.

Paul was longing to see his spiritual children in Thessalonica. He says in 1 Thessalonians 2:19-20: "For what is our hope, our joy, or the crown in which we will glory in the presence of our Lord Jesus when he comes? Is it not you? Indeed, you are our glory and joy." His spiritual children were his glory and joy—his inheritance! Paul rejoiced like a winner receiving a garland of victory, or a victor's crown, when he thought of his spiritual children and grandchildren whom he would present to Christ.

I have photos on my phone of my children and grandchildren that I carry with me when I travel. They are my joy and my posterity! When I look at them, I know I had a necessary role to play in their being on this earth. Our spiritual sons, daughters and grandchildren are our spiritual posterity.

Restoring the New Testament pattern

Although for the past 1,700 years much of the church of Jesus Christ has strayed from the truth of relational restoration between fathers and sons, the Lord is breathing a fresh word to His people. Rather than putting the focus on meetings and buildings which promote programs to encourage the spiritual growth of believers, He is calling us back to being His family and returning to the New Testament truth of building families.

Many believers are meeting house to house in small group throughout the world because the Lord is restoring this sense of family to the body of Christ. Christians are again beginning to relive the book of Acts. They are seeing the importance of empowering and parenting the next generation.

Parachurch organizations have understood this truth for years. Ministries like the Navigators, Cru (formerly Campus Crusade for Christ) and Youth With a Mission applied Ephesians 4:16 in their operations and found that if believers are trained, the body of Christ will expand. "From him the whole body, joined and held together by every supporting ligament, grows and builds itself up in love, as each part does its work." The body of Christ is meant to intricately fit together like the human body. When all members are working, the body of Christ will be healthy and grow.

Jesus wants His church to be restored to the New Testament pattern of family life. He ministered to the multitudes but focused on a few. These disciples changed the world!

True spiritual fathering and mothering was modeled by Jesus when he chose and trained his twelve disciples. Spiritual fathering and mothering and making disciples is basically one and the same. But when we understand spiritual fathering and mothering, we care about the persons we are mentoring while training them to make disciples at the same time. Persons we disciple are not our projects. They are people we love deeply and desire to see grow into their God-given destiny.

There are three keys to healthy spiritual fathering and mothering:

1. Initiating the relationship

2. Building the relationship and encouraging their lives

3. Releasing them to do the same thing

1. Initiating the relationship

Jesus initiated the relationship He had with the first disciples (Luke 5:4-11, 27-28). He took a season of time to watch the lives of those whom He was in relationship with before choosing His closest disciples that He called apostles.

...isciples left everything to follow Him, but it wasn't until
... a time of prayer (Luke 6:12-13), that He chose the twelve
...ciples. So start on your knees in prayer. The Lord will con-
... , the Holy Spirit, to the right person or persons who will
become your spiritual children.

Remember, the relationship must be mutual. There needs to be a sense on both sides that God is asking for a mutual investment in the relationship for a season. "Do two walk together unless they have agreed to do so?" (Amos 3:3). Love will need to be the pivotal point of the relationship. In addition to training them, Jesus also wanted to fellowship with His disciples relationally. "He called the twelve that they might be with Him" (Mark 3:14).

2. Building the relationship

Jesus healed many people and taught many people. But in the midst of what seemed to be a "busy ministry," He also taught His disciples to do what He was doing (Luke 6:17-20). As spiritual parents, we must be pro-active in building relationship. Getting to know someone takes intentional effort.

In this process, it is important to discuss each other's expectations. We can explore questions such as these listed below:

- What are both sides looking for?
- How often will we meet?
- Are there already certain areas of life and ministry that the spiritual son or daughter needs to grow in?
- How often should the relationship be evaluated? Start with a shorter term relationship and re-evaluate to avoid a situation where expectations are not being spoken or not being met.

Create an atmosphere of trust and respect. A spiritual son or daughter needs to be assured of the love of the spiritual parent. Allow that son or daughter to be free to be him or herself, without fear of judgment or impatience.

This trust and freedom is caught more than taught. Informal interaction models the kingdom of God by showing how Christianity works in real life. We provide on-the-job training. The goal of spiritual parenting is to increase your disciple's effectiveness in the kingdom of God. Take them along with you when you minister to others!

3. Finally, releasing them to reproduce

Jesus sent His disciples out and expected them to reproduce themselves (Luke 9:1-2,10). We will know when it is time to release a spiritual son or daughter. We need to release the next generation to build their own "homes" and reproduce.

Here is an example of how spiritual reproduction works. Take your spiritual son or daughter with you when you baptize a new believer. The next time, allow the son or daughter to do the baptizing as you assist. When the next opportunity to baptize comes, tell your son or daughter to find someone else to train and simply watch from the sidelines. Finally, the son or daughter will be comfortable enough to reproduce himself or herself in this area and will not even need your physical presence. They have learned to train others and reproduce themselves.

Remember, although we usually focus on Jesus' relationships with His twelve disciples, He also had a group of seventy-two disciples. We also see Him with an inner circle of Peter, James and John at certain times. Within this group, John was the disciple that Jesus seemed to love the most. John refers to himself as the "disciple that Jesus loved" five times in the book of John. Jesus clearly had different levels of relationships. You will be closer to some of those whom you disciple than you are to others. And that is acceptable. This is how it worked in the life of Jesus.

Thirsting for new wine

I believe the Lord is preparing to pour out His Spirit and bring revival to the church in these last days. The new wineskins, or church structures, of the early church were simple: people met from house to house. I believe our Lord's strategy to prepare for the harvest is still the same—He wants to use common ordinary believers who have encountered an extraordinary God to meet together as spiritual families from house to house to disciple, train and prepare for the harvest.

Many Christians today are thirsting for this great influx of new wine—new believers pouring into His kingdom. God is placing a desire within spiritual fathers and mothers to welcome these believers into the kingdom and then train them as spiritual sons and daughters. Small groups of believers meeting together provide an ideal structure for this. The micro church is meant to be a spiritual family with the leaders and other spiritual moms and dads in the group taking responsibility to train the spiritual children. Micro churches produce mature Christians in a family-like setting.

Although micro churches and micro church networks are wonderful wineskins for spiritual parenting, in themselves they are not the answer. It is not the structure itself that is significant, but the relationships occurring within its perimeters. If the people in the micro churches do not practice spiritual parenting, their groups can quickly become as boring and lifeless as any other structure. The life comes from the Lord and from the active discipling relationships that are taking place.

Our inheritance of spiritual children

This promise of spiritual children is for every Christian! God has placed us here on earth because He has called us to become spiritual fathers and mothers in our generation. With this comes the expectation that our spiritual children will themselves have spiritual children, and that this cycle will continue to produce more children into infinity.

Our inheritance will be the spiritual children that we can some day present to Jesus Christ. No matter what you do—whether you are a homemaker, a student, a worker in a factory, a pastor of a church, or the head of a large corporation—you have the divine blessing and responsibility to birth spiritual children who will in turn make disciples who make disciples. We are all called to impart to others the rich inheritance that God has promised.

I like how Abraham responded when the Lord showed him the stars in the sky and promised him descendants as numerous as the stars: "Abram believed the Lord..." (Genesis 15:6). What did he believe the Lord for? His inheritance! We, too, need to "believe the Lord" for many spiritual children. We can trust God to do it. It may not happen overnight, but it will happen when we trust in God's faithfulness. God wants to give us an inheritance of spiritual children, and He will do it through the generations. He is a God who has a heart for families and is concerned about the generations to come.

You can be a spiritual parent

Perhaps you feel you have already tried to be a spiritual parent but failed. Trust God for grace to start again. Someone once asked Mother Teresa what she did when she got discouraged because she did not see immediate results. "God does not demand that I be successful," she said, "God demands that I be faithful. When facing God, results are not important. Faithfulness is what is important." [3]

Maybe you never had a spiritual father or mother. You can give someone else what you never had by being his or her spiritual parent. You do not need to be perfect, just faithful and obedient. If you and I wait until we think we are ready to be perfect parents, we might never be parents at all.

Are you expecting the believers in your small group or micro church to become spiritual fathers or mothers? If not, you need to change your way of thinking. Many will become future small group leaders, elders, church planters and apostolic leaders as they fulfill their roles as spiritual parents. In the small groups and micro churches, they can experience "on the job training." This occurs through participation and modeling. In micro church networks, small group leaders are called by the Lord to become spiritual parents to believers in small groups within the micro church while elders and pastors become spiritual parents to small group leaders. Apostolic leaders become spiritual parents to elders and pastors who lead micro churches.

There is a tremendous need for spiritual parents in the church today. I can still hear the desperation in the voice of a dynamic young leader in New Zealand who opened his heart to me a few years ago. "I need a father," he stated. "Where are the spiritual fathers today?"

Jesus took twelve men and became a spiritual father to them for three and a half years. He knew that Christianity was caught, not just taught. He ministered to the multitudes, but most of His time was spent with these few men. His disciples changed the world.

By our Lord's example, we can do the same.

Notes

1   Matthew Henry's Commentary in One Volume, (Grand Rapids, MI: Zondervan, 1960), p. 119
2   Bobb Biehl, *Mentoring*, (Nashville, TN: Broadman & Holman Publishers, 1996), p. 19
3   Mother Teresa, *In My Own Words*, Compiled by Jose Luis Gonzalez-Balado, (New York, NY: Random House, 1996), p. 40

CHAPTER 8

Learning from History

The primary focus

The primary focus of a micro church should be outreach and discipleship, not merely fellowship. Great fellowship will be a healthy by-product of the micro church that is consistently reaching out to others.

When prayer and interaction take place within the group, needs will be met and relationships forged. That is definitely needed. But the top priority of a micro church must always be to bring in the lost. This will cause the micro church to mature and reproduce another micro church. It will give more believers the opportunity to use the gifts the Lord has given them.

The greatest catalyst for spiritual growth in Christ is taking our eyes off ourselves and looking to Jesus and the needs of those around us. A group of people who are always looking inward, content with the status quo, will not grow or multiply. Looking inward prevents growth. Like an ingrown toenail, it usually causes pain. Often, competition and stagnation result.

When micro churches are content to stay the same, without knowing it, they build walls around themselves that cause others to feel unwelcome. The group that has a heart to reach out will be willing to change, and will enjoy meaningful fellowship in the process.

When I was newly married and a young missionary, I heard a man of God quote C.T. Studd, the famous missionary: "I do not wish to live 'neath sound of church or chapel bell; I want to run a rescue shop within a yard of hell." These words were life-changing for me. The main purpose for every micro church must be to rescue people from the brink of hell. Otherwise, it becomes a social club without any power. The Lord gives us power to be witnesses, not to sit around and enjoy nice comfortable "bless me" meetings. The Word of God reminds us that we are given power to be His witnesses. "But you will receive power when the Holy Spirit comes on you; and you will be my witnesses in Jerusalem, and in all Judea and Samaria, and to the ends of the earth" (Acts 1:8).

The church is not primarily a hospital, but an army. Although armies have medical units, the purpose of these units is to get the soldiers healed and back on the battlefield in order to destroy the enemy. The focus is not on the medical unit. The focus is on winning the war.

We are in a spiritual war! We do not have time to sit around and play "church" as if we are children who are playing games. We need to rise up in faith, be the church, and destroy the works of darkness in Jesus' name.

When I was a young man, our nation was in the midst of the Vietnam War. Every year, comedian Bob Hope would take an entourage to Vietnam to entertain the soldiers. Now, let's face the facts. No one joined the army to see Bob Hope! They went to fight a war. However, while they were there, they had the fringe benefit of being entertained by Bob Hope and his company.

Although the primary purpose of the micro church is to reach the lost and disciple new believers, we also experience the fringe benefit of tremendous fellowship and relationships with people who care about us. They stand with us as we face hardships and struggles.

There will be many different creative approaches to reaching the lost and making disciples as we work together in a micro church setting. However, the primary vision must be clear and fixed—we are called to fulfill the Great Commission. We don't necessarily fulfill the Great Commission by listening to an evangelistic teaching or by going out on the streets to evangelize week after week.

When individuals in micro churches challenge each other to reach beyond themselves to make disciples, they will discover that God will give them many creative opportunities. Even if no one immediately comes to Christ through these opportunities, there is a spiritual dynamic released that keeps our focus on the harvest fields instead of on ourselves. As we continue to sow, we will eventually reap.

New churches provide more opportunities for evangelism

Let me remind you again of what Dr. Peter Wagner told us for years. "The single most effective way to evangelize is to plant new churches."

Fuller Theological Seminary found in a study that if a church is ten or more years old, it takes eighty-five people to lead one person to Christ. If the church is four to seven years old, it takes seven people to lead one to Christ. If a church is less than three years old, it takes only three people to lead one to Christ (see diagram below):[1]

Age of church	People/salvation ratio
10 years + old	85:1
4-7 years old	7:1
3 years & under	3:1

New churches give the opportunity for more people to come to faith in Christ. Let's plant new churches all over our communities, and reach more people for Jesus!

The Methodist revival

I have had the privilege of proclaiming the gospel on six continents. Amazingly, in nearly every nation I visit, I find a Methodist church building! Some of my Methodist friends tell me that many of these buildings serve as memorials to a past revival. What happened?

John Wesley, the founder of the Methodist church, saw that new wine must be put into new wineskins. He started "class meetings" to disciple the new believers being saved during the Methodist revival. A key to the revival was the accountability that the believers found in the small groups, according to Howard A. Snyder, in *The Radical Wesley*:

The classes were in effect house churches...meeting in various neighborhoods where people lived. The class leaders (men and women) were disciplers.

The classes normally met one evening each week for an hour or so. Each person reported on his or her spiritual progress, or on particular needs or problems, and received the support and prayers of the others . . . According to one author it was, in fact, in the class meeting "where the great majority of conversions occurred."

The class meeting system tied together the widely scattered Methodist people and became the sustainer of the Methodist renewal over many decades. The movement was in fact a whole series of sporadic and often geographically localized revivals which were interconnected and spread by the society and class network, rather than one continuous wave of revival which swept the country. [Classes joined together to form a society.]

Without the class meeting, the scattered fires of revival would have burned out long before the movement was able to make a deep impact on the nation.

Now here is the remarkable thing. One hears today that it is hard to find enough leaders for small groups or for those to carry on the other responsibilities in the church. Wesley put one in ten, perhaps one in five, to work in significant ministry and leadership. And who were these people? Not the educated or the wealthy with time on their hands, but laboring men and women, husbands and wives and young folks with little or no training, but with spiritual gifts and eagerness to serve.

The system which emerged gave lie to the argument that you can't build a church on poor and uneducated folk. Not only did Wesley reach the masses; he made leaders of thousands of them.[2]

Gradually, however, the Methodist believers put more emphasis on the weekly church meetings in their buildings than on the class meetings in small groups. As they de-emphasized the accountable relationships found in their class meetings, the revival movement began to decline.

I often ask the Lord to keep us from making the same mistake in this generation! We can learn from history that small groups and micro churches have often served to fan revival.

Back to the homes

Peter Bunton, in his book, *Cell Groups and House Churches: What History Teaches Us,* mentions that Martin Bucer, a key figure in the Reformation of the church in the 16th century, advocated a radical church reformation to begin in small groups or Christian communities:

> Indeed, he taught that partaking in such little communities modeled on the New Testament was the only way to keep the Ten Commandments.
>
> Additionally, what is of interest is that each group remained connected to others. The leaders were to meet each week, and every one to two months there should be a meeting of all groups in the parish for teaching. (This has some semblance of the structure that Wesley was to establish some two hundred years later!)[3]

Peter continues to clarify, "The ember that has rekindled movements of renewal ever since [the first century] is the cell group or 'micro community'.... As we seek to ignite a discipling movement in our own time, we must place the local prayer and support group concept at the very center of our strategy. The great reformer Martin Luther proposed that widespread spiritual renewal should take the form of *ecclesiolae* in *ecclesia*—little churches within the church."[4]

Throughout history, many movements have emerged to bring the church back to what it was in the first century. The micro church vision is a radical reformation of church structure that fits the New Testament practice of believers meeting in homes. Remember, the early church only started to erect their own buildings more than 250 years after Jesus' death and resurrection.

Once church buildings were put up, believers met in them for the greater part of their church experience. For centuries, the church has become accustomed to Christians gathering in a church building every Sunday, and it is hard to break the mold. However, tradition for tradition's sake gets us in trouble because we begin to trust a method rather than the Living God. Even micro church networks become legalistic and traditional if we trust the method or structure rather than allowing God to keep us flexible and open to His leading.

Jesus said of Himself, "For the Son of Man has come to seek and to save the lost" (Luke 19:10). Any and every church, be it a micro church, community church or megachurch, needs to take Jesus' reason for coming to earth as the reason for her existence, as well. When we do so, other elements of church life as a caring community of believers in Christ will fall into their appropriate places.

Notes
1   "Enlarging Our Borders," Report presented to the Executive Presbytery, January 1999
2   Howard A, Snyder, *The Radical Wesley*, (Downers Grove, IL: Inter-Varsity Press, 1980), pp. 53-57, 63
3   Peter Bunton, *Cell Groups and House Churches: What History Teaches Us*, (Lititz, PA: House to House Publications, 2001), p. 14
4   Ibid, p. 13-14

CHAPTER 9

Simplicity and Unity

The church in the New Testament was so simple that the common people gladly received the Word of God and met in homes, enjoying the Lord's presence and their newfound spiritual family life. They gladly suffered persecution, because Christ had revolutionized their lives.

Years of traditions since those early church days have made the church so complicated. God is calling us back to the simple gospel and the simplistic New Testament church.

My friends Dirk and Hanneke Develing from Apeldoorn, Netherlands, gave up pastoring a vibrant community church a few years ago to start a new micro church network. They told me recently:

Small churches are like a family gathering. They are fun, informal, relational and easy-going. Because they are small, it is easy to make changes and make decisions; you do not need to go through a complicated process.

These groups are easy to multiply. Most people who participate can see how it works and start a new micro church themselves. We just need to be sure the gatherings do not become sermon-oriented. If we don't keep things simple, then starting a new micro church becomes a more difficult task.

Another advantage of a micro church is that a small meeting does not require a lot of resources. A house or café is adequate—and it is good to have some good coffee, too. No fancy equipment, sound system, worship band or projector are required. In this way, the church does not get caught up with 'doing' church (programs, events, productions, maintenance), but can focus on simply 'being' church as a family. This means there is time left for doing ministry outside the church. The key is to keep it simple.

Psychologist Larry Crabb, in his book *Connecting*, remarks:

> Maybe the center of Christian community is connecting with a few, where ordinary Christians, whose lives regularly intersect, will accomplish most of the good that we now depend on professionals to provide. That will happen as people connect with each other in ways that only the gospel makes possible.[1]

We desperately need those relational connections in church life We need to empower every believer to be a minister. In healthy, thriving micro churches, people's lives easily and regularly intersect. In these places of commonality and relationship, believers can minister effectively to one another and even to their neighbors. Francis Chan in his book, *Letters to the Church* says it well, "We've strayed so far from what God calls church. We all know it. We know that what we are experiencing is radically different from the church in Scripture. For decades, church leaders like myself have lost sight of the inherent mystery of the church. We have trained people sitting in the pews to become addicted to lesser things. It's time for that to change."[2] New micro churches are a part of the Lord's plan for the future of His church in our generation.

Remember, micro churches are real churches

I have spent the past forty years involved in small group-based church ministry, and I believe in this structure for church life more than ever. However, we should again make the distinction between small groups and a micro church.

First, the small group-based community churches or megachurches usually have their own headquarters and administrative systems. Because of the small group-based structure, they encourage the real spiritual life to happen in small groups, usually in a home. But overall, these churches tend to be more meeting-centered and need a lot of administration to keep the various ministries and components running smoothly. Micro churches, on the other hand, require no headquarters. They are much more flexible and fluid because they meet solely in homes or other suitable locations and do not require another building for additional church programs.

Second, in the small group-based community churches or mega-churches, small group leaders do not have complete authority as elders of their groups in the way that they do in micro churches. Instead, small group leaders are an extension of the leadership of the elders of the local church in which believers meet each Sunday in a larger church gathering.

Micro churches are very different because they are self-contained churches in themselves. Each micro church has elders (with one of the leaders assuming the primary leadership role of the leadership team) who serve as spiritual fathers and mothers with a desire to train and reproduce more leaders within the micro church. This kind of fatherly or motherly leader gently nurtures individuals until they are ready to take a step of faith to become leaders themselves.

As already mentioned, a micro church usually includes several smaller "cell groups" within it. These groups often meet outside of the regular micro church meeting time, or might meet within part of the designated meeting time of the micro church. Smaller groups within the micro church often help to foster deeper relationships and greater accountability as people become involved in a lifestyle of everyday community. The micro church models a way of life. It does not carry the mentality of religious meetings. Church is people—living their lives in an extended spiritual family as they focus on reaching the lost. Although families require some organization, the type of organization in a family is relational, not bureaucratic.

Downsizing in order to grow

Downsizing is a familiar term in the corporate world. Corporations that face increasingly stiff competition in the global economy often need to downsize in order to stay afloat. Corporations that downsize are trying to rid themselves of unessential costs and liabilities. They may downsize their work force or inventory in order to cut unnecessary costs. This is one way they can continue to exist and realize profits.

Community churches, megachurches and micro churches in a region would do well to work together to utilize all their resources more fully. Why not "downsize" by sharing resources? I believe we will discover myriads of ways that churches, like corporations, can "rid themselves of unessential costs and liabilities."

For example, I look forward to the day when we can be so flexible that church buildings in our communities will be utilized every day of the week. Many community churches and megachurches currently use their buildings for a few choice meetings such as the Sunday morning worship service or midweek prayer meeting, and the church facility remains unused the rest of the week.

How about this scenario: a community church or megachurch offers, or rents, their facilities to several different micro church networks that want to meet together occasionally in a larger space. The micro churches could meet on Sunday nights or on a weeknight when the community or megachurch does not need its facilities. That would be divine efficiency! Money that is saved on constructing new buildings and maintaining old buildings could be given to missions and to the poor.

It sounds fairly simple, doesn't it? Is it asking too much for churches to work together like this? Perhaps we have taken the simple gospel and complicated it. Let's get back to the simplicity of the gospel and the simplicity of relational church life.

Healthy micro churches will network

There should be a natural desire for micro churches to network with other micro churches for encouragement and accountability. If you are living in a rural area and starting a micro church, find ways to reach out and network together with others in your locale. Perhaps the Lord will show you where to connect to a micro church network that shares your spiritual values. Maybe the Lord is calling you to start your own micro church network.

Most, though not all, micro church networks are networked regionally. Some micro church networks are small, with only a half dozen or so micro churches involved in the network. Others are much larger, with teams of apostolic leaders providing encouragement, oversight, and spiritual protection.

Micro churches that are not open to becoming a part of a micro church network often focus inwardly, become stagnant and lose sight of the harvest.

Of course, not all micro churches and micro church networks are the same. Although some are healthy, others are unproductive, reactionary and exclusive. Many times, micro churches will take on the personality and the value system of the primary leader. When you are involved in a micro church, it is important to know and trust the integrity of the person leading the group and to be in agreement with the values, beliefs and practices of the group.

Micro churches need leadership

One of the questions I am asked repeatedly is: "Do micro churches and micro church networks need leadership?" The answer is "yes." They need servant leadership. They need fatherly and motherly leadership. But they always need some form of godly leadership. If God's appointed leader does not give proper leadership, then the enemy will be sure that someone else, who is not God's appointed leader, does. The early church as described in the book of Acts definitely had leadership. Elders were appointed in every church. While teamwork in leadership is so important, God does call a particular person to be the primary leader of a team.

In the book *The Cry for Spiritual Fathers and Mothers*[3] I explain how leadership works in the local church in a way that honors the Lord, honors leadership, and honors the people being served. When a micro church says they have no need for leadership, the person voicing this the loudest is often the real leader who just does not want to admit that he or she is in charge! I am embarrassed by what I have seen in some micro churches that claim there is "no leadership," but I am also bothered by the autocratic, heavy-handed leadership I have seen in some community churches, megachurches and micro churches.

According to Hebrews 13:17, we need to obey and submit to leaders who "keep watch over us." They bring spiritual protection to our lives. We cannot try to blot out this truth from the Bible just because unfaithful spiritual leaders have abused it. Obedience and faithfulness to our leaders, however, must always be based on a higher loyalty to God.

I have the privilege of serving as International Director of DOVE International, an international apostolic movement. I am blessed to have spiritual leaders, fathers in the faith in the greater body of Christ, to whom I have submitted myself. Their input into my life brings great security to me and to the leaders with whom I serve.

True apostolic leaders will faithfully serve micro churches

All the churches in the New Testament were submitted to apostolic leaders. Paul tells Titus in Titus 1:5 to appoint elders in every city. These micro churches were given apostolic oversight by Titus who served on Paul's apostolic team.

Timing is paramount when it comes to finding an apostolic leader or leaders to serve a new micro church network. I have friends who lived on the South Island of New Zealand who experienced a move of God in their micro church. Within a few months, literally dozens of people came to faith in Christ and joined their church. The leaders of the micro church saw the need for proper connection in the body of Christ and for spiritual oversight. Watchman Nee once said, "We do not have authority unless we are under authority."

So, when my friends heard about an "apostle" who was coming to town, they assumed they should join with him and the other micro churches to which he was giving oversight. However, it did not take long until they realized he was actually a "wolf in sheep's clothing." Since he was not under authority, there was no one in that movement they could appeal to. Within months, the precious work of God in this micro church was in shambles because of the abusive "apostle."

Paul warns us against false apostles who are not fathers but who have a personal agenda. In reference to his spiritual parenting he said, "And what I am doing I will continue to do, in order to undermine the claim of those who would like to claim that in their boasted mission they work on the same terms as we do. For such men are false apostles, deceitful workmen, disguising themselves as apostles of Christ" (II Corinthians 11:12-13).

A micro church should be sure to take enough time to find true apostolic spiritual oversight. True apostolic leaders are accountable to other spiritual leaders in the body of Christ. God has called us to serve with humility and walk together in unity.

Unity: One church, many models

"They will know we are Christians by our love." The words to a popular 1970s church camp song rings true in any day and age. Today more than ever, people are looking for a church where people love each other and reach out to those different from themselves. The world is attracted by Christians who truly love each other. Jesus required it of true disciples: "A new command I give you: Love one another. As I have loved you, so you must love one another. By this all men will know that you are my disciples, if you love one another" (John 13:34-35).

Jesus knew that the love and unity of His believers sent a compelling message to unbelievers. With this in mind, He prayed for all believers in John 17:20-23: "My prayer is not for them alone. I pray also for those who will believe in me through their message, that all of them may be one, Father, just as you are in me and I am in you. May they also be in us so that the world may believe that you have sent me. I have given them the glory that you gave me, that they may be one as we are one: I in them and you in me. May they be brought to complete unity to let the world know that you sent me and have loved them even as you have loved me."

Jesus does not pray for His followers to "become one," but rather that they may "be one." The present subjunctive used here in the Greek designates ongoing action: "continually be one." This oneness is based on a common relationship to the Father and the Son, on having the same basic attitude toward the Word and on understanding the need to reach out to the lost. [3] As believers, we will "be one" if we continue to be in unity with God and each other. Unity breaks down barriers!

I believe the Lord is doing an awesome thing in our day. He is restoring the unity He prayed for in John 17:21: "That all of them may be one, Father, just as you are in me and I am in you. May they also be in us so that the world may believe that you have sent me." Walls that have divided denominations and churches for centuries are coming down at an increasing rate. Pastors in the same town who never knew one another are now finding each other, praying together regularly, and supporting each other. This kind of church unity is exciting!

The regional church

Unity like this makes room for the regional church to emerge. What is the regional church? It is a group comprised of all types of churches—community churches, megachurches, and micro churches —in a particular geographical area. These churches, of many different denominations, will work together to represent the church, the body of Christ, in a region.

In the New Testament, each church was identified by its geographical location—there were no denominations back then! The body of Christ met in micro churches within a city, and they were unified by their specific city boundaries: the church of Antioch, the church of Corinth, the church of Jerusalem, the church of Smyrna. However, today, the church has been divided into many different denominations within one geographical area. Many times, things such as doctrinal interpretations and worship styles have caused these divisions in the body of Christ.

The awareness of the regional church is not an attempt to do away with denominations and go back to organizing believers exclusively on the basis of geographical regions. I believe we have to work with what we have today. This means that the local churches within a collective regional church will probably each maintain their denominational flavor, but can work in a unified manner to share Christ more effectively. In short, when unbelievers see the unity of churches in their community, they will be attracted to the Christian faith experience.

Spiritual fathers and mothers unify to lead the regional church

Over the next years, I believe there will be an emergence of spiritual leaders from various backgrounds and denominations who will form teams of spiritual leadership to "father" this collective, regional

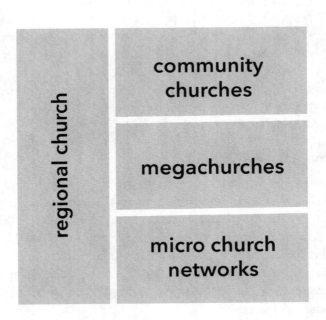

We need community churches, megachurches and micro church networks to work together.

church. These apostolic fathers and mothers will serve the church in towns, cities and regions. They will not think only in terms of pastoring a church or churches, but will sense a responsibility, with other fellow servant-leaders, to pastor their region and resource the body of Christ.

This initiative will not be contrary to their denomination's vision, but will bring wholeness. Although these "fathers and mothers of the region" will be concerned about unity, it will not be their focus. Their main focus will be on the Lord and on His mandate to reach the lost. Again, the regional church will include all the types of churches in a geographical location. All denominations and church movements operating in a region have a redemptive purpose from God to meet the needs of that particular region.

Churches in a region will honor each other

When LaVerne and I were married in 1971, we found we had two sets of relationships to pursue and maintain: those on her side of the family and those on my side of the family. Both were important. Similarly, we need to maintain healthy relationships with the spiritual leaders of our church movement, and we also need to keep healthy relationships with the spiritual leaders of our region. Each church and ministry in our region is to be honored. As we walk together in unity, the Lord will command a blessing.

God is bringing people of various backgrounds and affiliations together in unity. God is using these divine connections to accomplish His purposes. I believe God calls Christians from community churches, megachurches, and micro church networks to serve together as the regional church in every city in every nation. Together, we can reach our world for Jesus!

We still have much to learn

A pastor of a megachurch in our region asked me recently, "How does the micro church network fit into the regional church the Lord is restoring in the regions of the world?" My answer is that it fits like a hand in a glove since it is just another model of church. The only way it will not fit is if the micro churches become independent and refuse to work with other church expressions. This would be tragic.

Just as we can see and understand only a little about God now, as if we were peering at His reflection in a mirror, we have much to learn about micro church networks and the expressions of unity through the regional church. Although our vision is still a bit hazy, I believe we will soon see things more clearly. "The path of the righteous is like the first gleam of dawn, shining ever brighter till the full light of day" (Proverbs 4:18).

Earlier, I mentioned the dawn of the home school movement. In the beginning, only a handful of resources were available to home schoolers. Today, however, there are hundreds of resource centers that assist home school teachers and students. Similarly, as more micro churches are started and the regional church begins to emerge, I believe we will find increasingly healthy models to emulate.

Notes

1   Larry Crabb, *Connecting: Healing Ourselves and Our Relationships,* (Nashville, TN: W Publishing Group, 1997)

2   Francis Chan, *Letters to the Church,* (Colorado Springs, CO: David C. Cook, 2018)

3   *Full Life Study Bible,* NIV, (Grand Rapids, MI: Zondervan Publishing House, 1992), p.1621

CHAPTER 10

Planting and Leading
a Micro Church

Micro churches are being planted worldwide by ordinary people who trust in an extraordinary God and desire to obey the Great Commission. It requires faith to plant a new church. We might feel insecure, unprepared and fearful of the unknown, but a step of faith is necessary. Without faith it is impossible to please God. Our God rewards faith.

Pluman and Maya and their adult daughter, Liubomira, live in Sofia, Bulgaria. A few years ago, they took a step of faith and obeyed the call to plant a new church in Sofia. They rented a building from another church in Sofia for Sunday evening meetings. Members of small groups that were gathering at other times during the week would come together Sunday evenings for a joint celebration service. Throughout that year, they led people to Christ, but found that some were not fitting into the church they had started in Sofia. Instead of trying to force them into the groups that were already meeting, they wisely began new small groups. The small groups became micro churches for these new believers—new wineskins for the new wine. They used Discovery Bible Studies to train new believers how to study the Scriptures.

Many believers in the nations are doing similar things…starting new wineskins for the new wine of new believers. Micro churches are important new wineskins for the new wine of our generation. Perhaps the Lord is calling you to start, or help start, a new micro church.

Practical guidelines for starting a micro church

Let's get practical. If you sense the Lord may be calling you to be involved in starting a new micro church, it will be important to share this leading with persons you look to for spiritual oversight and counsel. Tell them that you are praying about involvement in a micro church.

Here are some guidelines regarding steps of faith you can take as you move in this direction.

1. **Pray, pray and pray for direction from the Lord.** Seek the Lord as to how He would want you to be involved in a micro church.

2. **Read** the book *House to House*, a vision-casting and training manual about starting and leading small groups and micro churches. Or read another book about micro churches that you feel may be helpful (See other recommended books in Appendix C). You can read the book on your own, or you can read it with a group and discuss together what you are learning.

3. **Focus on reaching new persons for Christ.**

4. **Disciple a new believer(s).**

5. **Help to lead a small group.**

6. **Lead a small group.**

7. **Train leaders in your new small group** who will assist you in leadership. They can be future leaders for the present group or the leaders for a new group they will start.

8. **Multiply a small group into two or more groups.** (The book *House to House* explains practically how to do this).

9. **Seek God for continued guidance about the next steps.** When you have experience with leading, training leaders for, and multiplying a small group, continue to pray that God will show you what your next steps should be. Discuss what you are sensing from the Lord with your church leadership.

10. **Seek the blessings of those to whom you are accountable** as you continue to discern God's will. Pursue God's leading. Discern if you are called to lead a micro church planting team, or if you are called to be a part of a team that will plant a micro church.

11. **Learn how to lead a Bible study** suitable for those who are not yet believers. The Discovery Bible Study[2] method, for example, helps persons engage with the Word of God in a personal yet non-threatening way and has been an effective tool for leading many into a relationship with Christ.

12. **Find ways to partner with others in this new vision.** Possibly join an established micro church in a network in your area if one is available. Or, meet with others who are called to plant new micro churches.

13. **Receive training**. Many tools for planting micro churches are available, including the DOVE Global Leadership & Ministry School.

14. **Build a micro church planting team,** or become a part of a team that is focusing on starting a new micro church.

15. **Develop a prayer base.** This could be a team of intercessors who will spiritually cover you in prayer.

16. **Discern where your primary spiritual oversight connection will be** when you plant this church.

17. **Discern possible mentors** for this new endeavor.

18. **Discern the Lord's timing with your team**, spiritual overseers and mentors.

19. **Pray for new people to come to Christ** and for laborers who will help you with the harvest (Matthew 8:38).

20. **Take a step of faith,** expecting the Lord to lead and bless you as you start a new micro church.

Responsibilities of a micro church leader

Every micro church leader needs to have a shepherd's heart. A person with a pastor's heart has a desire to serve a group of people through prayer, regular encouragement, and practical service.

The responsibilities of a micro church leader start with prayer.

In accepting to be a servant leader to a small group of believers, our first priority, next to maintaining a close relationship with Jesus and serving our families, is to pray for those the Lord has placed in our micro church. The prophet Samuel told the children of Israel, "As for me, far me it from me that I should sin against the Lord by failing to pray for you" (I Samuel 12:23).

Like anything else worthwhile, prayer must be learned, and learning takes time. Regardless of whether you feel you understand how to pray or you are still learning, micro church leaders are responsible to pray. This is the basic job description of a micro church leader; we are called to "stand in the gap" for both the saved and the unsaved. "So I sought for a man among them who would make a wall, and stand in the gap before Me on behalf of the land, that I should not destroy it; but I found no one" (Ezekiel 22:30).

One of the greatest ways to serve those within the micro church is to "labor in prayer" for them, according to Paul's description of his prayers for the Galatian believers. "My little children, for whom I labor in birth again until Christ is formed in you . . . (Galatians 4:19)." Ask God for direction and He will show you how to pray diligently for each person.

Since we are encouraged in Scripture to "pray without ceasing," I believe the Lord would be pleased if we purposed in our hearts to pray for each person in our micro church daily. We should also pray specifically for family members, friends, and acquaintances of those in our micro church who are unsaved. Some of my friends in New Zealand call the unsaved "pre-Christians." I like that. There is faith in that kind of terminology.

As the leader of a micro church, you also need to be involved in spiritual warfare on a daily basis. "Assuredly, I say to you, whatever you bind on earth will be bound in heaven, and whatever you loose on earth will be loosed in heaven" (Matthew 18:18). God has given you the authority to bind the powers of evil and to loose blessing and freedom in the name of Jesus.

Many people who are being manipulated by demonic spirits are not aware of this spiritual bondage. Paul explains this battle clearly in Ephesians 6:12: "For we do not wrestle against flesh and blood, but against principalities, against powers, against the rulers of the darkness of this age, against spiritual hosts of wickedness in the heavenly places."

When people are manipulated by demonic spirits, they may simply seem disinterested or unresponsive to what is going on in the micro church. In reality, the enemy is hindering them. When praying for the people for whom we are spiritually responsible, it is important that we pray in Jesus' name against any divisive spirits that would try to hinder our micro church from fulfilling its purposes in God. As a micro church leader, you need to "get in your prayer closet" and pray for them in Jesus' name, taking authority over any demonic spirits that are holding them back.

If someone is struggling with a life-controlling problem or openly displaying demonic activity, it is usually best for leaders of the micro church to meet with this person outside of the formal meeting. As you serve people in prayer behind the scenes, your group will experience more unity of spirit and a better atmosphere for spiritual growth. This will give opportunity for further prayer, counsel, ministry and deliverance. In areas of deliverance from demonic spirits, it is best to minister two by two whenever possible.

Praying the Scriptures has been a helpful way for me to pray. When you pray the Word of God, you can be assured that you are praying the Lord's will. Personalize verses with the names of those for whom you are praying. For example: "I pray that (Sam's) love may abound more and more in knowledge and depth of insight . . . " (Philippians 1:9-11). Other excellent scriptures to use in praying for spiritual growth among those in your micro church can be found in Colossians 1:9-12, Ephesians 1:15-21, and Ephesians 3:14-19.

As a leader, you will set the standard in prayer. Some time ago, I asked the Lord how to establish a church that prays. He spoke clearly and said, "You pray."

In order to keep pace and be accountable in prayer, it is important to have someone to pray with whenever possible. Jesus said in Matthew 18:19, "I say to you that if two of you agree on earth concerning anything that they ask, it will be done for them by My Father in heaven." Pray with your assistant leader(s) on a regular basis. This will help keep all of you alert to any hindrances that may arise in the micro church. Pray also with those who oversee you in your micro church network.

Some micro churches find it helpful for each person in the micro church to have a prayer partner. This may be changed monthly or from time to time. Other micro church leaders delegate prayer for certain individuals to different members of the leadership team so as to be sure everyone is covered in prayer daily. Prayer teams for spiritual warfare are also effective. Small group prayer is important because it helps us to know the heart of others; this fosters spiritual intimacy and strengthens relationships.

A few years ago, LaVerne led a micro church made up of mostly new believers. She met each month with the small group leaders that she had trained. This gave her the opportunity to pray with these small group leaders and train them to pray, so they in turn could pray for those within each of their small groups.

Remember to pray with expectancy! As believers in Jesus Christ, we pray with confidence that the Father hears us and will answer our prayers. Philippians 1:6 teaches us to be "confident of this very thing, that He who has begun a good work in you will complete it until the day of Jesus Christ." We should pray this truth for those in our micro churches and for those the Lord is drawing into His kingdom.

If your micro church seems to be lacking in the area of prayer, invite someone in who has an anointing in that area. Prayer is contagious. As you pray with someone who has a "spirit of intercession," your entire micro church will begin to experience power in prayer. Praying together will also help bring unity to the micro church.

Called to encourage, not control

One of the lessons to be learned from history is that micro church leaders who are immature or insecure may seek to control God's people rather than encourage them to hear from the Lord for themselves. Our goal must be to present every believer mature in Christ. "Him we preach, warning every man and teaching every man in all wisdom, that we may present every man perfect in Christ Jesus" (Colossians 1:28).

We need to help the believers in our micro church learn how to receive direction from the Lord themselves, not to depend on us to tell them what to do. Issues that are not clearly answered in Scripture should be left to the conscience and discernment of each believer. For example, a micro church leader should not be the one to make decisions concerning things like family finances, family size, child rearing styles, political differences, one's standard of living and so on. A leader can give counsel based on his or her understanding of the Word, but should avoid becoming "the voice of the Lord" in such situations.

Training at all levels

At the start of a new micro church, the micro church leader should pray for one assistant or several assistant leaders who will serve with him or her. On-the-job training can be done with several assistants at the same time. A scriptural method for training, whether it be for leading people to Christ or church leadership, is found in II Timothy 2:2: "And the things that you have heard from me among many witnesses, commit these to faithful men who will be able to teach others also."

The micro church then becomes the basic training center for all kinds of ministry. Missionaries do not suddenly and miraculously become trained overnight and leave for foreign fields. They can get training and practice in their micro church. Job training for leadership must include a hands-on situation. The first qualities to look for in an assistant are faithfulness, humility, and the willingness to serve.

This book you are reading can used as a resource for leaders to train new micro church leaders and new small group leaders. My book *House to House* is also a manual for training micro church leaders. The

DOVE Global Leadership & Ministry School is an excellent online comprehensive ministry training school God has used to equip present and future leaders from many church backgrounds and from many nations. More details on this school are provided in chapter 15.

The most important part of training future leaders, however, is still the one-on-one training that takes place when a potential micro church leader is discipled and trained by the micro church leader or assistant leader. The most effective training is on-the-job-training. A leader in training can go along with a micro church leader when he or she goes into the hospital to pray for the sick, or join in when he or she is meeting with someone who is discouraged. It has been a unique joy for me to lead others to Christ when I am with another believer who joins in as a prayer partner or apprentice. In this way, the miracle of a new birth unfolds right before his or her eyes. Jesus set the pattern for on-the-job-training. He spent most of His time training a few men, not teaching large crowds. God wants us to train others to train others who will train others … and keep the training cycle alive.

Micro church leaders in training need to understand clearly the scriptural principles they learn from training courses, as well as from on-the-job-training. They will need to be grounded in the Word in order to teach others. Practically speaking, it is best for a future micro church leader to be regularly involved in micro church group functions and in personal ministry in the small group setting before beginning to minister as a micro church leader.

Assistant leaders

Those who lead small groups within a micro church assist the leader in many ways. They are like a teenager who might "mother" a younger brother or sister—but doing so does not make that sibling the true mother. Later on, that person will be a parent and have his or her own children. This same principle applies to those who are pastoring people as leaders of small groups within a micro church. Small group leaders serve alongside a micro church lead elder (pastor) so that every believer can and will learn how to become a minister. We are all called to be ministers (Ephesians 4:12).

An assistant micro church leader has specific responsibilities to both the micro church leader and the micro church members themselves. Their responsibility in prayer involves not only involves praying with, but also for, the micro church leader. An assistant could serve as the leader of a smaller group within the micro church, and should be willing to serve in any other ways that are needed so that the micro church succeeds in drawing people to Christ and carrying out discipleship. In the absence of the leader, this assistant will give leadership to the group. He or she should look for ways to assist the leader by praying for and with people, discipling, encouraging, and serving in practical ways. An assistant leader will also bring any areas of concern, potential problems, needs or "blind spots" to the attention of the micro church leader.

In addition to serving the micro church leader, the assistant, will diligently pray for those in the micro church. He will help the micro church leader to contact individuals regularly by phone or in person to comfort, strengthen, and encourage them. Some practical ways of serving may include providing rides to meetings as needed, giving information to micro church members, and giving special care to new believers.

Set the example

In the micro church setting, the enemy will lie to us at times and tell us that we cannot really help others because we have not "been there." Was Jesus ever on drugs or alcohol? Was He ever divorced? No, of course not, yet He set an example for us to follow. Regardless of our backgrounds, we can pray and trust the living God and see the Lord do miracles among us.

You can set the example by sharing your own personal needs and problems with those in your micro church. The Bible tells us in II Corinthians 12:9 that we should boast in our weaknesses so that the power of Christ may rest upon us. When we are transparent about areas of struggle that we've had and how the Lord has given us grace to conquer by His Word, it keeps us from being placed upon a pedestal by others. When we allow people, perhaps without realizing it, to exalt us as being somehow "better" or "perfect," we open ourselves to the enemy in the area of pride. People we are serving feel as though they can never attain our level of spirituality, which is totally untrue.

We can minister most effectively by showing the people in our micro church the Word of God rather than by giving them our own opinions. If you don't have the answer, don't fake it. Tell them honestly that you don't know, but you will find the answer. That's why God provided network leaders and other ministry gifts in the body of Christ.

Remember, the Word of God gives us spiritual authority. Also, your testimony is a powerful tool that the Lord can use to encourage others. In your testimony, you simply share what God has done in your life in the past, what He is doing in your life now, and what you are believing He will do in the future.

Leaders should not give strong advice or correction to a person they do not know very well (unless they are clearly led by the Holy Spirit). Much patience is needed before attempting to correct someone's faults. Simply continue to love and care for them, and many times they will come to you for advice and help at a certain point. They will see in you an example of how they themselves want to be.

True leaders will take time—all the time that is necessary—to build good, trusting relationships with people. We must build relationships not only within the setting of the micro church meeting, but outside the meeting as well. Through informal time spent in social interaction, the time will come when you will feel free to speak into the lives of the people in your micro church because of the trust that has been established. If you don't have a relationship with the people in your micro church, it will be very difficult for them to receive advice or correction from you.

It is also important to be organized, perhaps using the task list on your phone, an appointment book, or some other type of daily reminder to help remember appointments and to arrive on time. To forget an appointment with someone gives them the impression that we don't really care.

Micro church finances

Micro churches receive tithes and offerings to be used to extend the kingdom to God. Micro church leaders make final decisions regarding the use of church finances. However, they need to be open to both the micro church members as well as network leaders regarding how the finances are being distributed. Most micro churches have a basket available during micro church meetings and the money is then counted by two persons in the group for the sake of accountability. It is preferable if those counting the money are not the leaders, but in small micro churches this is not always possible.

In cases where people are committed to both a micro church and to a community church or megachurch, a portion of their tithe can be given to both churches. This often happens when a missionary has a home church but is also involved in a mission church. They give to both.

In cases where a great deal of money is needed for a crisis, and it is beyond that which the local micro church can handle financially, other micro churches in the micro church network can sometimes help meet the need. This is the blessing of being a part of a network.

In the next chapter, we will consider more logistics about what happens in a micro church meeting and how those meetings can be led.

CHAPTER 11

Healthy Micro Church Meetings

In a micro church setting, Christianity becomes practical. Members grow in spiritual maturity because they learn to accept and love one another unconditionally. It's a place where believers pray for each other in their brokenness and witness the healing work of Jesus. The micro church setting becomes a workshop for learning about serving, accountability, prayer and worship. Compassion flows abundantly. A lesson for one becomes a lesson for everyone in the context of vulnerability and openness. As micro church members watch over one another, everyone grows stronger in Christ.

Although the specifics of every micro church vary, the dynamics of a micro church meeting are often different from those of a community church or megachurch weekend meeting.

Many pastors and micro church leaders have asked for details about what should happen in a micro church meeting. Although I am hesitant to give guidelines because every group will be different, I will in this chapter share basic ideas about practical aspects of a micro church meeting. The most important guideline, however, is to be truly open to the Holy Spirit and follow His lead.

How many people should be in a micro church?

Jesus' micro church consisted of twelve disciples. Moses encouraged small groups of ten. Ten to twelve adults seems to be an ideal number of people to serve together. However, new micro churches only need a few people to start. If two or three gather in His name, He is in their midst (Matthew 18:20). When the group grows to twenty or more, it can become too large to be effective. Having said that, however, I have noticed that others prefer up to seventy in their micro church as long as they have small groups within the micro church for discipleship and leadership training. The key to starting new groups is leadership. If leaders are not adequately prepared to start a new micro church, it is best to wait until they are. People who are involved in micro churches without clear leadership often become disillusioned.

Sometimes when a micro church becomes large, another unforeseen problem arises. Where do you park all the cars when you meet together as a micro church at someone's home? If the overflow spills onto the side of the street, it can be a potential problem for neighbors. In this case, we suggest that micro church members car pool whenever possible. The community should always be respected.

Choosing a location

When deciding where your micro church will meet, the following are some things to consider. Is the location central for the majority of the people in the group? Does it have enough room for the group to gather and share freely without interference? Is there enough privacy? If needed, is there a separate room for children's ministry? If in a home, does it offer a comfortable and relaxing atmosphere to adults and children as well? Are the hosts financially able to meet the needs that hosting a group involves? Or, is the cost of renting an office space or other location affordable for the micro church?

It has been common for micro churches to meet in the same location—usually a home but sometimes other venues like an office or coffee shop—until a group multiplies or a change is required. However, some micro churches have found it more advantageous to rotate the meetings to various homes or offices of the micro church members. Those who are willing to host the meeting find it to be a special blessing!

Persons in a micro church have the opportunity to share life experiences openly with others in the micro church. This often includes having a meal together, although this is not required. If the group is sharing a meal, the host should not be the one to provide all the food. Everyone should be encouraged to bring food to micro church meetings.

Meeting time and format

Most micro churches meet once a week, but others have found it more effective to meet together every other week or even once a month. In the case of less frequent micro church meetings, times of outreach or smaller small group meetings can take place during other weeks. Sometimes micro churches will alternate a regular meeting with an outreach or game night. Sometimes the women will meet separately from the men on the off weeks. Since relationships are one of the priorities in the micro church, believers should be spending time together in various settings.

Micro church meetings often include a time of worship, testimonies, a short teaching, time for response to the teaching, announcements, prayer, and sharing of life together. The format can be changed and altered in a thousand ways. You do not have to do all of these things, or in reality you do not need to do any of these things. Every time you come together should be different. Do not get stuck in a rut. I once heard that a rut is a grave with the ends knocked out. Doing the same thing week after week hinders fresh life from flowing in your micro church.

Unless you are clearly led otherwise, I encourage you to keep the meeting to about one to one and a half hours. Have a schedule and stick to it, unless you know that the Holy Spirit is leading otherwise. Make sure you start and stop your meetings on the agreed times, unless the Holy Spirit clearly leads you in a different way. Be respectful of other people's time, especially parents of babies and young children.

Preparing well for the meeting is so important. Many times we say we are "following the Holy Spirit" when in reality we have been lazy and are unprepared. This is a disgrace to our Lord and to His people. It is a sign of poor leadership to waste people's time. It is important to always be well prepared!

The time following the meeting is full of opportunities for sharing and meeting the spiritual needs of the people. This is often the most important time of the micro church meeting. Those who want to seek help from the micro church leader or others in the micro church are free to do so. Many times after micro church meetings, small clusters of people may gather together informally to share heart to heart and pray together. These times of fellowship are invaluable as fellow believers surround one another with compassion and prayer and gain the courage to keep going and stand tall, embodying the very fullness of Christ (Ephesians 4:11-16).

Both in and out of the micro church meetings, remember your mission—to pray, reach the lost, and make disciples. Unless we keep our eyes firmly fixed on our mission, we will forget why we are getting together in the first place. The enemy will deceive us and put us asleep spiritually while the world goes to hell around us.

Teaching in the micro church

During a teaching in a micro church setting, members are usually free to comment and respond. It is helpful when messages include the opportunity for dialogue. If people in the micro church are largely new believers, the teachings will be different from those given among more mature believers who need to be motivated and stirred to win the lost.

Encourage those who teach to use modern day parables and stories that apply to the lives of God's people. Jesus constantly taught with stories. When people remember a story, they also remember the spiritual truth. A key to teaching is to be a good story teller. Some years ago, I developed an interest in Dwight L. Moody, the famous evangelist of the nineteenth century. I remember my amazement when I picked up a book of his sermons. They were filled with stories. John Wesley, the founder of the Methodist church movement, used to rehearse his sermons in the presence of his nine-year-old servant girl. If she could understand it, then he would give the message publicly.

Give others in your micro church the opportunity to teach from the Scriptures. This is especially true if you are a gifted teacher. Those in your micro church will think they could never lead a micro church because they cannot teach like you. They need to see you allowing others to lead according to their own personal spiritual gifts. Encourage those in your micro church to tell their story about their journey with God. Give them lots of encouragement.

The question to ask is: What will be the most effective thing for our micro church to do for every person to know Jesus in an intimate way and be equipped to fulfill the Great Commission? In answering this question, we have at times used sermon jams from the internet for the purpose of teaching. Some micro churches have used the DOVE Biblical Foundation Course as a teaching format for a season. Many love the Discovery Bible Study approach. If someone needs healing in the group or has a friend who is sick, perhaps there could be a short teaching on healing with a time of prayer for the sick.

It can be refreshing to invite someone with the gifting of an apostle, prophet, evangelist, pastor or teacher into a micro church meeting. These "circuit riders" can impart more under the anointing of the Holy Spirit in one meeting than you could imagine.

Most importantly, each group is encouraged to do whatever moves them most effectively toward the goal of reaching the lost and making disciples.

Worship leaders

If possible, each micro church should try to have at least one person designated to lead the group in worship. If a person is selected for this ministry, he or she does not need to play an instrument—although many do—but should be able to lead in worshipful singing unto the Lord. Many micro churches use YouTube videos for worship when there is no one in the group who is gifted as a worship leader. Whether using live music or something recorded, the worship leader should make song sheets available for any members who are uncomfortable worshipping without knowing the words. The worship leader should stick to the allotted time given by the micro church leader for the worship period.

Some micro churches do not have a time of singing but spend time in prayer instead. Micro church members can be encouraged to come to the micro church meetings with a song or a hymn to share. When everyone feels a sense of responsibility before the Lord for what happens at the micro church meeting, you can expect the Lord to move through His body in a powerful way.

Teach people to pray

Prayer should be a vital part of the time a micro church has together. Ask someone beforehand to open with prayer. Have a time for intercession and praise. Give everyone an opportunity to pray. Be helpful and encouraging when people are learning to pray out loud by using short, conversational prayers.

One of the men in a small group that I led a few years back was afraid to pray publicly. He knew that he had to deal with this fear. He told me to ask him to pray in front of the other men in the group in one of our morning meetings. As I asked him to pray and encouraged him, he went on to lead various groups in the years that followed. He just needed some encouragement and accountability.

Explain the importance of praying in agreement according to Matthew 18:19-20, "Again I say to you that if two of you agree on earth concerning anything that they ask, it will be done for them by My Father in heaven. For where two or three are gathered together in My name, I am there in the midst of them."

Maintaining order during the meeting

Keep the meeting moving and alive. Whoever has been given responsibility for a particular part of the meeting must be enthusiastic so that people do not become bored.

If you feel that your meetings are getting out of hand because one person monopolizes the time, you may need to encourage that person who is overly verbal to stick to a time limit. This will ensure that others also have time to share.

If someone takes the meeting "down a side street" by getting off the subject, you can tactfully tell that person you will be happy to talk privately about whatever the "side street" is after the meeting. In this way you honor the individual and also keep the meeting from becoming boring for the rest of the people.

If there are those who constantly interrupt, they should be gently confronted with the truth that they need to "consider others as more important than themselves." I Corinthians 14:26 tells us, "What then shall we say, brothers? When you come together, everyone has a hymn, or a word of instruction, a revelation, a tongue or an interpretation. All of these must be done for the strengthening of the church" (NIV).

Nothing should be permitted to take place that does not line up with the Scriptures or that quenches the Holy Spirit. For example, one evening I was leading a small group meeting when one of the men began to "pray" in a tongue that sent chills up my spine. There was something drastically wrong. I turned the meeting over to someone else and along with another Christian brother took this man into another room to minister to him. It became apparent that he needed deliverance and the voice he was "praying" in was the voice of a demon.

Call people by their names

In North America, it is the cultural norm to use first names when talking to people. In this context, it is important to know the people in your group on a first name basis. Other nations and cultures may require us to use proper names or family names. Regardless of the specifics, however, we should draw out every individual and encourage each one to participate. When teaching the Word of God, use the names of the people in the micro church as often as possible when you give illustrations or parables. It makes people feel important—and they should—because they are definitely important to God!

Jesus, the Good Shepherd, knows each of His sheep and calls them by name. As the micro church leader spends time in prayer for each member on a daily basis, it will not take long to remember each one's name.

In case you have difficulty remembering names, here is a helpful tip: when meeting someone and hearing his or her name for the first time, think of someone else you know who has the same name. It could be the name of a friend or family member or a character in the Bible. Then make the mental connection to help remember the name every time you think of the new person until you have it memorized.

Don't put people "on the spot"

While we want everyone to participate in the micro church meeting, caution is needed so that we do not embarrass anyone by having them read Scripture, pray, or explain a verse if they are uncomfortable with this. If you want someone to give a testimony, ask them about it beforehand. You may know some people well enough to know they will be glad to participate in these ways. But if you are not sure, ask them before the meeting and give them the freedom to decline. Encourage timid Christians to be open, but speak with them privately about their participation first.

I have a family member who was "put on the spot" in a Sunday School class as the class members were taking turns reading the Scriptures one person at a time. This family member had difficulty reading and was so uncomfortable and embarrassed that it took twenty years for her to gain enough courage to go back to a Sunday School class. A sensitive leader could have saved her a lot of pain.

These introverted or shy people are best reached by gaining their confidence outside of the formal meeting. If there is someone who sits in the corner and hesitates to join in, make a point of spending time with that individual in casual conversation a few times and gradually enlist him or her to take part in the meeting and activities.

Be flexible and creative

Don't settle into a dull routine; keep the meetings vibrant. Plan in advance for new activities. Talk with other micro churches to find out what they are doing. Ask the people in your group periodically for suggestions.

On occasion, when someone in the group has a need, you could all go to their home to help them instead of having the regular micro church meeting. One night when our micro church was together, we realized that the one couple was missing because they had fallen behind on their yard work. Rather than condemning them for missing the micro church meeting, we laid aside our plans for the meeting and went to their home to help them. We all had a tremendous time and were able to minister to the couple in a practical way.

Water baptism

It is God's will for new believers to be added to the church daily! When Peter was speaking to a crowd of Jews in Jerusalem, he finished by saying, "Repent, and let every one of you be baptized in the name of Jesus Christ for the remission of sins; and you shall receive the gift of the Holy Spirit" (Acts 2:38).

When a new believer comes into a micro church, the micro church leader should inquire if he or she has ever been baptized in water. If not, plan for a baptism. Network leaders are usually available to give training on baptism when needed. They also can help the micro church leader find a suitable location. We have used swimming pools, bathtubs, rivers . . . anywhere where there was water available for a baptism.

Take this opportunity to teach new believers the purpose of water baptism from the Scriptures. Water baptism signifies our "death" in Christ and our "resurrection" with Him into new life as we come out of the water. Romans 6:1-10 provides a relevant text from which to share the gospel at the water baptism site.

Often the entire micro church and the person's family will attend a baptism. This provides a great opportunity for witnessing and celebration. Sometimes the new convert will give his or her testimony during the baptism. Be sure to have a time of prayer for anyone who is being baptized. Many times, words of prophecy will come forth for these believers.

Communion and love feasts

Each micro church has the liberty to celebrate the Lord's Supper as often as it wishes. It is a vital part of the Christian life to remember and meditate on the death and resurrection of our Lord Jesus Christ. Paul stressed it was the most important issue he could preach: ". . . Jesus Christ, and Him crucified" (I Corinthians 2:2).

A time of Holy Communion should be both reverent and celebratory, as the Holy Spirit leads. The leader can read or discuss passages such as I Corinthians 11:23-26, or passages from the gospels about the Last

Supper or the death and resurrection of Jesus. It can be very meaningful to have someone in the micro church sing a special song. Alternatively, background music could be played as communion is shared together.

Baby dedication

When a newborn is dedicated to the Lord, it is a special time for the entire group as well as for relatives of the child who may not be a part of the micro church. It can be a time of joy and a powerful witness. The group should affirm their willingness to help the parents in training the child for the glory of God.

Sometimes the micro church leader will read the story of baby Jesus' dedication found in Luke chapter two, and allow the parents to express their commitment to bring up the child in the nurture and admonition of the Lord. This scripture from I Samuel 1:27-28 is also meaningful during baby dedication: "For this child I prayed, and the Lord has granted me my petition which I asked of Him. Therefore I also have lent him to the Lord; as long as he lives he shall be lent to the Lord."

What about children in micro churches?

The Lord values children. They can take an active role in micro church life because they are part of the spiritual family. The Bible says, "Jesus called the children to him and said, 'Let the little children come to me, and do not hinder them, for the kingdom of God belongs to such as these'" (Luke 18:16). Remember, children are the church of today!

Children need a vital relationship with Jesus at their own developmental level. Faith development is a process occurring alongside the other aspects of growth. A micro church can offer children a spiritual home and family; a place to belong. In the micro church, children have the opportunity to express love and gratitude to God through worship and praise. Discipleship can also take place in this safe and loving environment. Seeds are sown in children's lives which will bear fruit. Micro churches can also be lots of fun for children!

We have found that when new believers with children come to our micro church meetings, they may find it hard to focus while trying to take care of their children. In many cases, it works better for them if there is some type of ministry available for children.

In whatever form the ministry to children takes, it is important that we be aware of the need to protect the children in a micro church. Child abuse has reached shocking proportions. Statistics now tell us that one out of every three girls and one in seven boys will be sexually assaulted before they reach the age of eighteen. In this regard, some micro churches require a background check for anyone who works with children. When more people have a background check, there will be more options for who can be called upon to help with the children as needed. For the purpose of accountability, it is advisable for two people to minister together to the children, unless they are all within sight of the larger group of adults.

Parents and micro church leaders could have many different preferences regarding how to minister effectively to children in their micro church. Some micro churches gear the entire meeting to the family and have the children with them the entire time. In other micro churches, children are involved with their parents for part of the meeting and then have their own activities and ministry the rest of the time. Creativity and flexibility are the keys to providing fellowship and teaching for children in micro churches.

There are many creative options for children in the setting of a micro church. Here are a few specific ones.

Family participation plus separate children's ministry time

Many micro churches in North America prefer to include children in part of the meeting, and have a separate children's ministry time as well. Children are incorporated into the time of worship, testimonies, and prayer, then receive their own ministry in another room in the home or perhaps in a neighboring home, if appropriate.

There are several options for who can minister to the children when they meet separately. Various micro church members could take turns ministering to the children on a rotating basis. Older children can minister to younger children. Parents could take turns ministering to the children. A team can be formed using only one parent from a family so the other parent can attend the meeting. This will help keep unity and continuity in the micro church.

Total family participation

In the option of family participation, children are with their parents for the entire micro church meeting. The teaching and worship are geared to the children, and families learn together. Supplemental ministry to parents might be added by an occasional men's breakfast or ladies' outing.

Basic child care

Another option some parents prefer is to hire a baby-sitter for their own younger children. This gives the parents a "night out." They can receive uninterrupted ministry and learn to minister to others while their children are being cared for.

Children's ministers from without

In some cases, someone who is not a member of the micro church comes in to minister to the children during the micro church meeting. Either an offering is taken for the children's minister at each micro church meeting, or some of the money from the micro church tithes can be used to pay the children's ministers.

Micro churches serving each other.

Some micro churches share children's resources with one another. A person with a call to children's ministry could minister to the children in another micro church that meets on a different night than his or her own church.

Micro churches with no children's ministry

Some homogeneous micro churches of senior citizens, youth, singles or married couples without children may not need to have a children's ministry at all. Couples with children should not get involved in a micro church of this type unless the church is ready to adopt and incorporate ministry to children in the meetings.

One micro church we were involved in had the children with us for the entire meeting twice per month. In these meetings, the teaching was geared towards the children and they were involved in the discussion. For the other two meetings of each month, there was a special children's ministry for the children in another room at the home where we met. It worked out very well.

Here is one mother's experience with children in a micro church:

All the kids in our group stayed with us. We ate a meal together, took communion together, sang together—the kids often requesting their favorite songs. After singing, one family would do an activity they had prepared that often was a "hands-on" activity or game that offered a godly message or teaching for the kids. The adults would join the kids in this activity (singles and teens too!). Afterwards, when individuals began to share in the meeting, the kids were given the chance to read any Bible passages that we discussed. Otherwise, the young ones could draw or color while they remained in the room with us, sitting on the couch, snuggled with a parent, sprawled on the living room floor. Of course, much of the discussion went over their heads! They're kids! But they were with us throughout most of our time together, and were permitted to be kids. One of the families had a swimming pool and sometimes we would hold our gathering on their back patio and let the kids swim and have fun together. Now here's the thing: they loved our times of fellowship, and the children all felt like they were extended family with one another—brothers and sisters. They looked forward to any time we got together with any of the other families and had little difficulty communicating with either adults or other kids. When visiting families came, their children were welcomed without reservation.[1]

Micro church social activities

Social activities in the micro church group help to further build relationships. Outings, civic tasks, serving others, eating together and local evangelistic outreaches are just a few examples of the kinds of activities in which a micro church can participate. It is not necessary for each activity to include everyone in the group. Believers can get together for a baseball game or for a craft session. These are great activities to reach those who do not know Christ.

People who are gifted in the area of organization may be assigned to help plan activities. Delegation of responsibility gives people a sense of kinship for what God is doing. Remember, micro churches are called to be teams, working together to build the kingdom of God. And please do not forget, our primary focus needs to be prayer, discipleship, and reaching the lost.

Micro churches can also meet for breakfast or for a meal during a day off or over a lunch break. Another option is to combine activities for the entire micro church or for a portion of the network. Before finalizing any plans for a combined event, though, it is best for micro church leaders to check with their network leaders to make sure this event does not conflict with another function of the micro church network.

Birthdays and anniversaries

Birthdays and anniversaries are an important part of our lives. Some of the believers that the Lord has placed in your micro church may not have a family who cares about them, or their families may live in another state. Remembering birthdays, anniversaries and other special events with cards, gifts or an occasional party can be a tremendous source of encouragement.

It would be a good idea for someone in the micro church to compile a list of addresses, birthdays and anniversaries that can be given to the entire group. As the micro church grows and multiplies, this list will need to be continually updated. But the information about those who have moved on can still be used as relationships continue even after micro church multiplication.

In all these guidelines, remember that a micro church meeting is not intended to be a miniature Sunday morning community church meeting. The micro church, instead, is to be a safe environment for the Lord's people to share their lives together, pray, share the Word of God, make disciples, and receive a vision from the Lord to reach the lost.

Notes
1   Homechurch.org, posted 05-18-2001, by Lisa C. from Florida

CHAPTER 12

The Nuts and Bolts
of Micro Church Multiplication

When we obey the Lord and step out in church planting, we are choosing a life of sacrifice. But experiencing the fruit of our labor is so rewarding. Jesus said it like this, "If anyone desires to come after Me, let him deny himself, and take up his cross, and follow Me. For whoever desires to save his life will lose it, but whoever loses his life for My sake will find it" (Matthew 16:24-25).

When Floyd McClung was pastoring Metro Christian Fellowship in Kansas City, he asked me to speak at his church and help train a few hundred small group leaders on a Saturday morning before the multiple weekend services. Floyd made a statement to his small group leaders that I will never forget. He said, "There are young leaders among us who will be planting new churches from our church. Many may be house (micro) churches, and some of them may not even be a part of our church. Maybe they will join with another movement. Regardless of where they serve, we must get behind them and help them." This is an honorable posture to take as the Lord prompts many believers to plant new micro churches and micro church networks right in our own back yards. They are needed; let's support them!

LaVerne and I have felt the Lord calling us back to our roots—helping to plant new churches in our own community. Nearly twenty years, ago we worked with a group of young leaders in our county to establish the Lancaster Micro Church Network. So many new believers were discipled during the ten years of this network's existence. When it became clear that there were no persons called to continue on with leadership of the network, we helped micro church members find other churches in our region. But we learned so much during this season of micro church ministry. So, a few years later, along with some team members eager to start a new micro church network, we formed a new DOVE ministry called the House to House Micro Church Network. This micro church network has focused on planting new micro churches, mostly in our community in Lancaster County, Pennsylvania. Today, eight years later, more than ten micro churches have already begun, with more in the pipeline. Two of these micro churches are in states outside of our home state. (More about the House to House Micro Church Network story is given in the next chapter).

We have found through the years that it is a natural tendency for believers to want to stay in the groups they are familiar with, be it in a small group, micro church, or even community church. However, if we can understand our Lord's heart to see new people come into His kingdom, micro church multiplication will be a great joy as the kingdom of God continues to grow through micro churches that multiply.

The multiplication process

When micro churches are committed to grow and multiply, many more churches can be planted.

The process of cell multiplication in human cells is called "mitosis." It is multiplication by division. One cell becomes two, and each continues to grow until they, too, divide and separate to become four cells. The growth continues. Similarly, each micro church and cell group goes through a period of gestation (growth and learning) before it can give birth to a new group. Remember, growth is healthy. A healthy church is a growing church in several ways: numerical growth through adding people to His kingdom and growth in maturity as people grow closer to our Lord Jesus.

For a new micro church, the first few months are a good time for sharing testimonies and building new relationships. Everyone could share how they were brought to the Lord, how they were baptized in the Holy Spirit, how they came to the micro church, or other topics of choice. It is very healthy to share these spiritual experiences. In this way, people begin to be knit together and understand more about each other. It also provides opportunities for deeper friendships to develop.

After a season of initial relationship-building, there should be more of an emphasis on bringing others into the micro church. Everyone should be encouraged to share with friends, neighbors, workmates, colleagues, and loved ones about Jesus and how He changed their lives. Trusting the Lord for at least two people or families to come to Christ each year is certainly not too high of a goal. Those who have no Spirit-led goals often have no vision. The Scriptures tell us that without a clear vision, we will perish.

The micro church leader needs to continually speak out the vision for multiplication. Then, as the group gets larger, people will begin to talk about birthing a new micro church. When the time is right for a micro church to multiply, nearly everyone will be ready for it because they were anticipating multiplication from the beginning.

I was a member of one group that became large and cumbersome. We decided to meet in smaller groups for prayer during our home group meetings. A month or two later we decided to take these four prayer groups and meet in separate homes. We were still a part of the same larger group, but we met at times as smaller prayer meetings in different homes instead of always attending the regular group meeting. After doing this for a while, some of the small prayer groups became so excited about their small prayer group that they decided to begin a new group. Multiplication happened! It is said that some people never learn to swim until they jump into the water. The same is true with micro church multiplication.

A lot of prayer and open communication are needed as changes can be seen coming in a micro church. People need time to get used to a new idea until it is birthed in their own hearts and they welcome it. When this happens, a change will not be traumatic, but something that everyone looks forward to with enthusiasm and faith. The micro church leader can invite every member to seek the Lord's wisdom on any proposed change and bring their feedback. It is best if a decision to multiply can be confirmed by as many people as possible in the group.

During this time the micro church leaders should be accountable to the network leaders who will pray with them and assist them in any way possible.

We are often asked how often a micro church should multiply. The answer depends upon what the Holy Spirit is saying in every specific situation and culture.

Sometimes a small group in our micro church has been praying for a particular town or area, and a few small group members or other micro church members who live there subsequently feel called to begin a new micro church in that town. Because assistant leaders have been raised up previously in the micro church, there is leadership potential to accommodate multiplication.

We must continually share the "why" of multiplication from the Scriptures to keep us from getting into a rut. The purpose for multiplication in the micro church and in the micro church small groups is to see God's people released to train others and fulfill God's Word (II Timothy 2:2) and fulfill the Great Commission (Matthew 28:19-20). The early believers walked in the fear of the Lord and in the comfort of the Holy Spirit and were multiplied (Acts 9:31). We are called to do the same.

Modern day circuit riders and micro churches

One of the secrets to John Wesley's Methodist micro churches and exponential kingdom growth were the circuit riders. These "fivefold ministers" were spiritual specialists who traveled from micro church to micro church. "It was he who gave some to be apostles, some to be prophets, some to be evangelists, and some to be pastors and teachers, to prepare God's people for works of service, so that the body of Christ may be built up" (Ephesians 4:11-12).

God is raising modern-day fivefold ministers in His church today. These are spiritual fathers and mothers called to train the next generation in their specific gifts and calling. Fivefold apostles, prophets, evangelists, pastors and teachers circulate within the micro churches to train and equip leaders. They speak with the Lord's authority because they represent one of the ministry gifts of Jesus Christ. The Lord sent these fivefold parents to us so that we might be complete, lacking nothing. The Lord validates them by the evidence of spiritual fruit, changed lives and supernatural signs following their ministry. They are recognized by local church leadership because they have nurtured their gifts under the authority and context of a local church.

How are fivefold ministers grown in the first place?

As an individual serves and allows God to shape his or her character, specific gifts and anointings become apparent. That person is then recognized and given greater responsibility. Experienced fivefold ministers will recognize these gifts and offer mentorship. In this way, the body of Christ is equipped, encouraged and brought to maturity.

Many of these fivefold ministry gifts are intended to bless the church in trans-local ministry, not solely one congregation or micro church as seen in Acts 15:22, 30-32, 35. These gifts should be far-reaching as they minister to every level of the church: individuals, families, small groups, micro churches, community churches, megachurches, movements, and the church at large.

Apostles, prophets, evangelists, pastors and teachers help the church come to maturity

Apostles are given to the church to help us receive a vision from the Lord to reach the world. Prophets are given to train us to listen to the voice of God. Evangelists are called of God to stir and train us to reach the lost. Pastors are commissioned by the Lord to encourage and show us how to make disciples. Teachers have a divine anointing to assist us in understanding the Word of God. Beyond this, many fivefold ministers also have a "gift mix." For example, someone may be a prophetic teacher or a teaching evangelist. The apostle, prophet, evangelist, pastor and teacher must learn how to function together in order for the church of Jesus Christ to come to a place of maturity.

Churches of all types need regular impartation from each of these ministry gifts, and micro churches have an excellent opportunity to receive this ministry and impartation. There are only so many megachurches and community churches to go around, and many community church and megachurch pastors prefer to do much of the preaching and teaching each Sunday. But micro church leaders tend to think differently. They are looking for specialists in the body of Christ who can come into their micro church and minister according to the gift that the Lord has given to the fivefold minister. This is why it is important for people with these various gifts to minister the Word of God in micro churches. For example, if your micro church is lacking zeal for evangelism, ask an evangelist to come and minister to you for a few weeks. Then see if any of the believers in your micro church are willing to go along with the evangelist to share their faith with an unsaved person. You will be amazed at the results!

Since a micro church does not have as many overhead costs related to building mortgages and maintenance and paying staff, they are able to give monetary gifts and love offerings to support these fivefold ministry specialists who come to help them.

Micro church networks and missions

Traditionally, western missionaries have had a tendency to export the only type of wineskin they have experienced. We have already noted that micro churches are the normal way to do church in many developing nations, particularly in areas where Christians function underground or experience persecution. Missionaries who are sent out of micro church networks will have a unique advantage in a foreign mission field. They have already have experienced basic Christian community and New Testament church life from house to house.

Micro churches also have a unique opportunity to be missional within their own communities. Cross-cultural missions can take place "at home" as micro churches ask the Lord to guide them into ways to serve immigrant populations, students from other nations, neighbors or local businesses.

Commissioning

Whenever someone in the micro church is going on a mission trip or mission assignment, the entire micro church should have a part in commissioning them. This commissioning should not take place on the spur of the moment. It should be announced well in advance so that no one is taken by surprise. During the time of commissioning, members can lay hands on the person or persons who are being commissioned, and as many as are led by the Lord should pray. At this time, prophecy and words of wisdom and knowledge may also be given.

Commissionings are also recommended when multiplying a new micro church or when confirming new micro church leaders or assistant leaders from within the group. Communication with the network leader prior to this is important. If the micro church network leader can be involved in the commissioning, it gives the Lord's people a sense of being linked to a movement of God, not just to a small group of people.

Dissolving a micro church

To maintain healthy micro churches, everyone should realize that the micro church will eventually need to multiply. Even so, there have been times when a group has been together for quite some time without multiplying and finds it hard to keep an outward focus. They are satisfied with their experiences of mutual support and forget their mission to reach out beyond themselves. The closer I look at my face in the mirror each morning, the more imperfections I see. The same principle applies to the church. If we just sit around and look at each other, we can quickly begin to dwell on the imperfections that we see in one another. This will inevitably lead us down a road of disillusionment and destruction in a micro church setting.

When a micro church leader and others in the micro church sense they have become spiritually stagnant and have no desire to multiply, they sometimes realize they must dissolve. It is important to have one of the local network overseers involved in the process of dissolving a micro church. These persons have the grace and experience to help micro church members quickly find their place in another micro church before the enemy can sow seeds of discouragement or confusion into their lives.

Sometimes when a micro church dissolves, it takes a period of time for believers to get involved in another micro church. The network leader may start a "transition micro church" that he or she leads temporarily to support God's people and help them discern their future church involvement.

Pitfalls to avoid in micro churches
Pride

A common pitfall to avoid in micro churches and micro church networks is pride. Micro churches are not the cure-all for today's ailing church. If those of us who are called to micro church networks take a superior attitude, the Bible tells us we will fall. Micro church networks are only one of the many ways God is building His church. We should never have an exclusive attitude.

Fear

Another trap to avoid is fear. Micro churches are largely unproven entities in today's church world in developed nations. They are new for this generation and depend on initiative being taken by grassroots leaders. But when stepping into the unknown, it is common to experience fear.

Within a micro church, members might be nervous about multiplying into new groups. Some might see this as a 'split' and be afraid of what lies ahead. In any of these scenarios, we have to learn to move in faith, not in fear.

Independent spirit

Still another hidden danger is developing an independent and isolationist spirit. Sometimes those who do not want to come under any type of spiritual authority will gravitate towards micro church ministry because they believe they can do their own thing without having to answer to anyone. This kind of independent spirit is a form of pride and can destroy the move of God's Spirit.

Heresy

Micro churches may fall into the trap of heresy if they are exclusive and unwilling to work with others. All this can be avoided by being accountable to other leaders in a micro church network and the body of Christ at large. We all need accountability to keep us from heresy.

In the next chapter we will look at various modern-day micro church networks that have sprung up in different parts of the world.

CHAPTER 13

Modern-day
Micro Church Networks

My wife LaVerne and I have been involved in various aspects of micro church ministry for the past twenty years. It has been a great blessing see micro church networks flourish here in the United States and in other nations. In this chapter we want to look at a few examples.

Various models of micro churches are emerging as new micro church networks take root in different communities and nations. Some micro church leaders prefer to use the term micro church and others use the term house church. Sometimes, these smaller churches do not only meet in homes but in other venues as well. But their vision and call from God is basically the same: train leaders to start new micro churches, focus on discipleship among new believers, and start new micro churches with these new disciples.

Micro church networks as a new wineskin

Brian and Kim Zimmerman from Lititz, Pennsylvania, started meeting weekly with several friends—reading through books of the Bible, talking, praying and growing in faith. Initially, Kim had been discipling three young women who wanted to learn more about how to read and study the Word. Their lives began to change. These young ladies were so excited that they would bring their friends to the Bible studies, then their husbands. With more people attending and coming earlier for the weekly meetings, they introduced the idea of having a meal together as part of the evening events. Soon, Brian and Kim realized this was actually a micro church. They called their new micro church Shift. By the way, we encourage eating together as a vital part of healthy micro church meetings if possible. It builds a sense of family among us.

Simultaneously, while this new group was experiencing church in a micro church model, a small group of us were serving with another couple, Chad and Chris Miller, to start a new micro church, The Gathering, also in Lititz. One of the many strengths of The Gathering was the various discipleship groups (small groups) that were started. Every other week after we ate and worshipped together, we met in these small discipleship groups in different rooms of the house. Many found healing and freedom and grew as believers in Christ in these small groups, and future leaders were trained.

With the planting of these two micro churches, we formed a new DOVE micro church network that is today called the House to House Micro Church Network. Over the next few years, leaders from The Gathering micro church were trained and sent out to start two new micro churches. The House to House Micro Church Network has now grown to over ten micro churches with more new micro churches on the horizon. These micro churches meet on different evenings throughout the week.

Each micro church is different from the others with its own call and personality. One micro church focuses on outreach in a local park in a nearby city at least once every month, while another micro church focuses on helping people find freedom and healing from emotional wounds. Other micro churches focus on other areas of ministry like feeding the homeless, discipling new believers in the Christian faith, or building a strong spiritual family. But the leaders of each micro church have a vision from the Lord to make disciples and train leaders who will also train leaders to start new micro churches in the future.

The network provides the registration with the government and spiritual and financial accountability for the churches in the network. The lead elders (pastors) of each micro church receive mentoring and spiritual oversight from one of the couples on the network leadership team. We call this network leadership team an apostolic council. This team gives leadership to the vision for the network. The apostolic council also meets with the lead elders of all of the micro churches one evening a month. We spend time praying for one another and sharing God's vision for the future as new micro churches are started. There is also a youth group for youth from the various micro churches since the micro churches are relatively small and youth need opportunities to connect with other youth.

Each micro church receives tithes and offerings and they each have their own bank account. Nearly all micro church leaders have a job or business that supports them and do not need to receive a salary from the micro church. This helps make funds available to help the needy in their church and community and give generously to missions. Remember, most micro churches do not have to spend on paying staff, buying a building or even paying rent. They are blessed to have money to give to bless others.

After the House to House Micro Church Network was established, the Zimmermans, who were leading Shift as mentioned above, began to disciple several young couples who were preparing to get married. But this was more than pre-marital counseling; it was a walk of mentoring and discipleship. After several years investing relationally into these unchurched couples, they requested Brian and Kim to start a church for them. So instead of inviting them to their micro church and multiplying a new church out from the micro church they already had, Brian and Kim felt led to begin a new micro church with these couples who had recently given their lives fully to Christ. One of the couples in the new micro church offered their house and they started Thrive micro church. This is the strategy we find in Luke 10. Do not always invite new persons to your micro church, but instead, pray for a person of peace and start a new church in their home.

The Zimmermans believe the heart of a micro church is relational, and works best with twenty or less people. They find that most participants prefer the smaller, more intimate settings. Keeping the groups smaller also works better logistically because it is often difficult to fit more than twenty people in one house comfortably. We also encourage micro church leaders to start small groups or prayer groups within their churches. Small groups that meet either during the meetings, or at another time, help future leaders to grow.

One of the initial micro churches, The Gathering, eventually closed, and the original leaders moved across the country to California.

This church fulfilled its purpose in God to reproduce two new micro churches that are thriving. The new churches have a call from God and a desire to reproduce again.

The focus of the House to House Micro Church Network is to make disciples and to train leaders who train leaders who train leaders (II Timothy 2:2). This is the strategy given to us from Jesus' Great Commission in Matthew 28:19-20. We are very excited about the churches that will be planted and the networks that will be birthed in the coming months and years through the House to House Micro Church Network.

Discipleship training school births a micro church movement

The Hive Communities is a DOVE micro church network in Corvallis, Oregon. Tim and Angie Wenger lead The Hive Communities, which includes three micro churches of about thirty to seventy people, each led by their own lead elder or team of elders. Church elders are responsible for developing a leadership team within their congregation and working with their team to nurture a unique micro-vision that fits within the overall vision. Once a month the three churches come together for a larger gathering.

When in their early twenties, Tim and Angie were members of a church that was transitioning into a cell church. Tim explains, "We found great fulfillment and success in developing the youth ministry totally around cell groups. Yet I realized that many leaders with a pastoral gifting were called to lead a larger number of people than those found in a cell group. Hebrews 13:17 became very meaningful to me as I pondered how to develop a church structure that would release as many elders (pastor-shepherds) as possible who had the authority, gifting, calling and character to 'watch over peoples' souls' and give an account for those souls before the Chief Shepherd. As such, I was drawn to house church networks."

But the Wengers did not start a micro church network at the time. Almost twenty years later, after being directors of a discipleship training school known as The Mandate, Tim and Angie sensed a call to church planting. They found others in the community who had the same passion. In 2010, The Mandate board members sensed God leading them to venture out in faith. They decided to sell their homes and relocate to a new town where they could work together in church planting. Several other individuals and families were led by the Holy Spirit to move from various towns in Oregon to be part of this church planting initiative.

"I personally struggled with doubt and fear," Tim remembers. "Are we hearing God correctly? What if folks sold their homes and moved, and it doesn't work out? Angie, along with other leaders in my life, were a constant source of support and encouragement and regularly affirmed that we were to move forward, despite the risk. We planted The Hive Communities in Corvallis, Oregon and joined DOVE International for our oversight." Corvallis is a college town with a population of more than 50,000. It has a large foreign student population, many from countries that are closed to the gospel of Jesus Christ.

When they started The Hive Communities, the team focused on what God was calling them to build. "It has been said that the seeds of success or failure of a church plant are sown in the first meeting. For us, we see that if a church planting group is focused on what they are against, they will fail. But if what God has called them to is built into the foundation, they will move toward success. Because micro church structure is unique and non-traditional, at times it can draw folks who have a negative attitude toward authority. We did not want to have an "anti-" attitude built into our foundation." For this reason, leaders of The Hive Communities asked God to deal with any such attitude in their own lives first. They then sought for functioning oversight in order to embed the principle of accountability into the community.

The Wengers identify several uniquely positive features of the micro church model where smaller churches network together. The structure of such a group is lightweight and easier to lead and reproduce than some other church models. Leadership development takes place naturally with the planting of new churches. An elder leading the church can also still work full time, eliminating the need for paid staff. Because of the size, churches can meet either in large homes or rented facilities. The small group size also means that everyone can participate in giving a Psalm, prophecy, or teaching (1 Corinthians 14:26).

Missions and outreach take a central place in this network. "A large part of our focus is to send folks to unreached places in the world that have never heard of Jesus," Tim explains. The Hive Communities is intentional about staying focused on connecting with non-believers and one-on-one discipleship. They seek to reduce activities that do not contribute to evangelism and discipleship and promote gatherings of twos and threes for accountability, discipleship and mentoring. They encourage worship that is participatory, celebratory and focused on Jesus, and find it helpful to teach through books of the Bible in each church.

Communal living is also an important aspect for many people in The Hive Communities. Tim and Angie, for example, welcome people to live with them and observe their lives. They see this as one of the most effective strategies for evangelism and discipleship. "God set the solitary in families" (Psalm 68:6).

Micro churches flourish in Asia

There are also micro church hybrids where churches and networks are starting both new micro churches and community churches. One of many examples is in a nation in south central Asia (names withheld for security reasons). In the context of Hindu domination, micro churches are being established in villages that have no other Christian church expression. These groups meet in homes. National missionaries will move into a village and find a way to effectively meet needs in the community. This could be through a water project, early childhood center, orphanage, provision for handicapped persons or vocational training initiative. Meeting practical needs helps the missionaries gain acceptance and the right to be heard. Relationships of trust begin to develop.

When at least ten adults have accepted Christ and have been baptized, the leaders transition from being missionary outreach workers to pastors, and the outreach is considered a church. There is an emphasis on finding a "man of peace" (Luke 10:6) from within the community to sustain and propel the spread of the Gospel. In fact, the conversion of a man of peace is usually the key for church growth.

These village churches often send prayer teams to a nearby lage with a focus on praying for a man of peace. By the time a churc grows to forty members, a new leader has already been identified. It is understood from the beginning that multiplication is part of the plan for the church. Churches multiply when they reach forty because they can no longer fit in a house. Before a convert to Christianity is given responsibility as a pastor or sent out as a missionary, however, one year of Bible School training is required.

Interactive Bible studies are used in these churches in smaller group gatherings called cell meetings. These small groups within a micro church meet once a week, again in a home, to read the Word and discuss it. Most of these groups have ten to twelve members. Other group meetings are held regularly during the week as well, such as those that would be typical in a community church. This includes special groups for ladies, for prayer and for youth.

While these micro churches are part of an apostolic network that plans for church planting and provides training, they are not able to meet together in large gatherings. This is different from many micro church networks that come together monthly or quarterly for joint fellowship. These micro churches do know they are part of a network, however, because there are no other churches or Christians in their area. They have a unique identity and sense of belonging in the family of Christ. They also have the privilege of coming together during the Christmas season. Christmas is acknowledged as a Christian holiday, and Christian churches are given unique opportunities to meet and even evangelize during this time period.

The growth of these micro church networks is very encouraging, especially because the churches are made up of believers who have converted from Hinduism or other traditional religions. They are an expression not only of new wineskins for the body of Christ but of genuine Kingdom expansion.

ches and training leaders in Myanmar

and his team oversee nearly eighty micro churches
hout Myanmar. He has trained a leadership team that
groups of house church leaders throughout their nation. He has
also started a leadership school to train leaders in Yangon.

The micro church model penetrates in Africa

I recently met leaders of a new micro church network in an East
Africa nation that is growing rapidly. Several of the micro churches are
made up of former Muslim believers.

In yet another East African nation, we are honored to partner with
a micro church leader and church planter who oversees a micro church
network of more than two hundred micro churches.

Micro churches in Latin America

Justo Llecllish oversees a micro church network of twelve micro
churches in the Lima region of Peru. Here is Justo's story.

"I always said that discipleship was the most important thing in our
church. But once I was confronted by my own words. My heart asked
my head: If this is true, why do Sunday services require more planning
and a larger budget than discipleship activities?

From there we started a church re-engineering. We wanted a
model that is totally focused on the Great Commission: making disciples. Period.

The day came, and we announced during a Sunday service that we
would start functioning as churches in houses. Everything would stay
as it was, except there would be no more Sunday meeting that brought
everyone together. Since we had small groups, we asked for them to
meet on Sundays.

We immediately noticed several wonderful results. First, the joy
of personal relationships increased, for now there was more time to
cultivate relationships. Second, we had an unprecedented evangelistic

reach, for all who lived in the hosting house participated in the meetings. That is, our leaders immediately had more than ten people in their care.

I will never forget what a young lady said when she saw her own family gathered in prayer: "This is the best thing that has happened to the family."

Since we had freed ourselves from the burden of producing weekly worship, we now had time to relate to people who previously attended our church, and also those who do not attend church at all. I used to think these people didn't want to know anything about God, but I was wrong. It was simply that my old church model was an impediment to effectively shepherding them.

When I visited them in their homes, some of them agreed to become hosts for a church at home. That caused us a holy challenge; we had to train more leaders to minister in the homes.

As I related to the unconverted, I realized that almost everyone had a history with the church. Perhaps they had attended a children's church, but then disconnected. I even found pastor's children who, although they did not live in immorality, simply did not attend a church.

I realized that there is a way to reach these types of people. I learned this when I met someone who had a schedule that conflicted with the meetings of a conventional church. I suggested to him, "Would you like to study the Bible with me?" He answered with a nice "yes." I remember we had discipleship times of up to five hours, and sometimes we had to stop simply because the cafeteria had to close.

I started encouraging my leadership team to do the same. We had to get un-used to small group "liturgies," and we turned to a strategy of coffee conversations. Jesus' statement, "For where two or three gather in my name, there am I with them" (Matthew 18:20), helped us shape this approach.

Literally, the gates of heaven were opened to us to start micro churches of two, of three, of families, of friends; inside the city, out of the city, even outside the country. What we lack now is more leaders!

After much prayer to the Father asking for more workers for His harvest, we are now executing a training strategy that includes both theory and mentoring. In this way, anyone can start a micro church, starting with their home. We will send them with an online discipleship tool whereby the ultimate goal of the discipleship will be to help them complete the online school."

Paul the apostle tells the Philippian believers, "In all my prayers for all of you, I always pray with joy because of your partnership in the gospel" (Philippians 1:4-5). It is our joy to see partner churches in the DOVE International family of churches and in the body of Christ following God's guidance to create new wineskins for new believers.

As individuals and churches continue to seek His face, I believe we can see every believer reach his or her full potential in Christ as the body of Christ partners together to fulfill His purposes. I am convinced we will hear many more "God stories" of new believers coming to Christ and new micro churches starting in the coming months and years.

CHAPTER 14

A New Model for
a New Time

You may remember the popular movie *Field of Dreams*. A farmer hears an "inner" voice and builds a baseball diamond in a cornfield, out in the middle of nowhere. Baseball legends mysteriously appear, and the fans flock in from miles around.

In the real world, in biblical history, God instructed His people to build by following a pattern. If they followed the pattern, He promised to come! In Exodus 25:8-9, God gives instructions for building the tabernacle. The tabernacle was to be a sanctuary or a place set apart for the Lord to dwell among His people: "Then have them make a sanctuary for me, and I will dwell among them. Make this tabernacle and all its furnishings exactly like the pattern I will show you." If we follow God's pattern, He will come, and in the process, release new kinds of structures or wineskins for the church. To be successful, the infrastructure of the church must be built according to God's pattern.

Paul the apostle says in the book of Acts, "The God who made the world and everything in it is the Lord of heaven and earth and does not live in temples built by human hands" (Acts 17:24). He lives within us. We are the tabernacle of God.

I believe we are living in the days of preparation and restoration. We need to listen keenly to the voice of the Holy Spirit, then do what He tells us to do. When the Lord pours out this new wine and awakens communities to the things of God, we must have the new wineskins prepared or we will lose the harvest. God is preparing us for the job He has for us to do. We are pressing on "...to take hold of that for which Christ Jesus took hold of me [us]" (Philippians 3:12). As we press on and determine to follow the pattern Jesus has set before us, He promises times of refreshing and restoration (Acts 3:19-21).

Understanding the purposes of God

God in His sovereign wisdom has a time and season for all of His plans. Over and over again in Scripture, we notice how God's people are often unaware of what God is doing or what He wants to do. When God sent the Messiah, many of God's people were blind to Jesus' purpose on this earth. Today, the church often does not discern when or how God is fulfilling His purposes.

In 1 Chronicles 12:32, the men of Issachar are mentioned because they had an understanding of the times and discerned what God was about to do, which was to bring David to the throne. "Men of Issachar, who understood the times and knew what Israel should do—two hundred chiefs, with all their relatives under their command."

The leaders of Issachar not only knew what Israel should do, they also agreed on how to do it. In addition, the leaders were in unity with the two hundred "relatives under their command." This group was not a large group, but their unity and oneness of purpose was invaluable in fulfilling God's purposes during this critical time in history.

The time is now to hear God's voice and join Him to fulfill His purposes here on earth. Rick Joyner, a prophetic voice in today's church, wrote in his Prophetic Bulletin that he believes a major awakening will soon occur within the church, and discerning leaders will be ready for it:

A revolution is coming to Christianity that will eclipse the Reformation in the sweeping changes that it brings to the church. When it comes, the present structure and organization of the church will cease to exist, and the way that the world defines Christianity will be radically changed.

What is coming will not be a change of doctrine, but a change in basic church life. The changes that are coming will be so profound that it will be hard to relate the present form of church structure and government to what is coming. The new dynamic of church life will overshadow the Great Awakenings in their social impact, transforming cities and even whole nations. It will bring a sweeping sense of righteousness and justice to the whole earth.

The future leaders of the church are now being given a vision of radical New Testament Christianity being restored to the earth. It is time to heed the call and allow the Lord to lead His people to the new wineskins that will be able to hold what is about to break out upon the earth. Whenever there is a choice to make between the new and the old, choose the new. To be a part of what is coming, we must have the faith of Abraham who was willing to leave the security of the known to seek God in unknown places. The future leaders of the church will be willing to risk all to seek the city that God is building, not man.[1]

A new pattern

I, too, believe we must "allow the Lord to lead His people to the new wineskins that will be able to hold what is about to break out upon the earth." Today, I have the same sense of expectancy about the new micro church networks that I had about small group-based churches taking their place as recognized expressions of church forty years ago. Many potential pastors are sitting on church pews and chairs today, finding no room for their gifts to be released in their present church structures. We must allow a radical kind of Christianity that becomes a life force to break out and motivate our future leaders to action.

Micro church networks enable the priesthood of all believers, and require no expensive church buildings. Every believer will begin to realize the part he or she will play in discipling the nations. As a result, I believe micro churches meeting in every community will cover our nation within the next few years.

Multiplying people and leaders is not that hard to do. Micro church leaders should continually speak the vision of growth and multiplication and the fact that healthy families expect their children to eventually grow up and start their own families. A good leader will focus his or her time and energy in training faithful, potential leaders. Most potential leaders do not think they have what it takes to be a leader. They need to be encouraged.

One time, in our church, we invited more than two dozen potential small group leaders to a restaurant, enjoyed a meal together, encouraged the potential we saw in their lives, and prayed for them individually. One year later, nearly all of them were serving in leadership in small group ministry.

Why are many future spiritual leaders who sit in church pews and seats every Sunday or who attend small groups unaware that they could be leading a micro church? It could be because the only models they have seen are the community church model and the megachurch model. But these are not the only models available.

I believe there are thousands of future micro church pastors who will have faith to lead twenty to seventy believers in a micro church as a spiritual father or mother, but they would never want to lead one-hundred-plus people and attempt to maintain the many programs and ministries—and possibly even a building project—that a traditional church often requires. The micro church network gives us another model for church and church leadership.

We need many more churches

We need more new wineskins in our communities! The micro church model gives more believers the opportunity to start new churches. Besides all the potential micro church leaders who are sitting in the church pews, I believe there are thousands of former pastors and Christian leaders who have retired or are now working in the marketplace, unaware that they could be starting a completely new church that will bring the message of God's love to more people. Many unsaved people will not enter a church building, but they will come into our homes or will meet in a designated venue that is not a church facility. Micro churches, led by humble spiritual moms and dads, are not only a wave of the future—they are also the need of the future!

Ericka Anderson explains in the Opinion page of the *Wall Street Journal* that we could actually be in a time of spiritual awakening in the United States, spurred on by the rise of micro churches:

> As thousands of churches close across the U.S., many fret about the inevitable decline of faith in American life. Congregational demise is troubling, but underreported data suggest that fear of a secularizing America may be overwrought. A religious renewal could be on the horizon.
>
> It's true that denomination-based churches—Methodist, Baptist, Episcopal, Catholic—have been on a downward slope for years. But nondenominational evangelical churches are growing in number, from 54,000 in 1998 to 84,000 in 2012, according to the Journal for the Scientific Study of Religion. One reason for the success of the new evangelical congregations is their aggressive pursuit of growth, which they call "church multiplication." A new church will commit to start several smaller churches in a short time. "House churches," composed of neighbors meeting for informal services—usually in living rooms—are on the rise as well...
>
> Complacency is dangerous, but it's important to realize that religion in the U.S. is far from dead. With a vibrant, new church landscape on the scene, there will be no shortage of options to choose from as millions of Americans again find their footing in faith. A selection of churches may be dying, but their replacements are alive, well and regenerating in ways the American church has never seen before.[2]

Micro churches will be diverse

As we have seen through the examples in this book, micro churches and micro church networks will not all look the same. There are many variations and hybrids.

Since micro churches are decentralized, they do not require a lot of organization and administration. To keep administration to a minimum, some micro church networks share an office in their city. Why have twenty copy machines when you only need one? In some micro church networks, the leaders of the churches give a tithe of the money they receive to the overseers of the micro church network in their area. In other micro church networks, the leaders give their personal tithe to those over them in the Lord. Others will do both. Still others have a looser connection with the leadership of the micro church network. Some micro church leaders prefer small churches of six to eight persons, while others feel it is more effective to have a church of up to seventy persons meeting in a home. Obviously, you need a large home or another venue for a group this large, but none of these models is exclusively right or wrong.

With all the new models and varieties on the forefront of kingdom expansion, it might be difficult to stay abreast of all the Lord is doing through those who follow His leading with obedience and abandon. Trying to explain what is happening, however, is not our task. We can trust that the Lord will have His way and rejoice in the fresh wind of His Spirit in His body, the church.

Notes
1 Rick Joyner, The Morning Star Prophetic Bulletin, "Revolution," May 2000
2 Ericka Andersen, "Thank God American Churches are Dying," https://www.wsj.com/articles/, Wall Street Journal, February 20, 2020

CHAPTER 15

Broadening
our Scope

Working together: community churches, megachurches and micro churches

All three kinds of churches working together will have a significant impact in discipling people and changing lives in our communities. Some community churches and megachurches will commission leaders to start micro churches and give them the oversight needed to help them grow. Other community churches and megachurches will "adopt" micro churches in their communities and help them network together. Still other community churches will commission future micro church leaders to join with micro church networks in their region. The fundamental idea is that our Lord's kingdom is being built and expanded in a particular region.

In fact, even though most micro churches will continue to birth new micro churches, some micro churches may actually become community churches. And some of these community churches could become megachurches. It is all up to the Commander-in-chief of the church, our Lord Jesus Christ. There is tremendous freedom in the kingdom of God!

During the industrial age, adults usually kept the same job their entire lives. But in today's information age, studies show that the average person will make at least five career changes during the course of a lifetime. Today's society is a mobile one that forces us to be flexible. This same principle applies in church life.

Some people may be in a micro church network for a season, and then be called by God to become involved in a community church or a megachurch. Therefore, it is important to keep open and friendly relationships with persons who are involved in church models that are different from ours. Each kind of church has its strengths and weaknesses as it endeavors to empower people for ministry.

What if I am not called to a micro church?

If you are reading this and have no interest whatsoever in becoming involved in a micro church network, my admonition to you is to obey the Lord and allow Him to use you in your community church or megachurch. But please guard your heart so you do not persecute the next move of God.

Over the course of history, the established church and even newer church expressions have often persecuted the next wave of God's Spirit. Early reformer Martin Luther persecuted the Anabaptists and had them placed in prison. I have heard some of my Assembly of God pastor friends lament that they persecuted the Charismatic movement of the 1960s and 1970s. The latter example is oddly amazing since both groups believed in the baptism in the Holy Spirit and the manifestation of spiritual gifts. They really should have been walking in harmony and supporting one another.

Likewise, the micro church movement will need to carefully guard its heart as micro church networks spring up alongside community churches and megachurches. The church of today is diverse, and diversity is healthy. God is working through program-designed churches, small group-based churches, community churches, megachurches and through micro church networks.

So how should those of us called to serve with community churches and megachurches respond to micro church networks that emerge in our community? Let's welcome them, reach out to them and offer them help to succeed. Many of these micro church networks may ask to rent our church buildings for their monthly or regular celebrations. This would be a win-win situation for everyone!

The Charismatic church did not replace the denominational churches of their day, but grew up right alongside more traditional churches. It seems ironic, but some believers today are leaving Charismatic churches and going back to churches that are more traditional. I believe the Lord smiles at us when we get too serious about these things. Those who call on the name of Jesus are everywhere and in every Christian church. Christ has set us free, and we are free indeed (John 8:36).

Broadening our scope

DOVE International, the worldwide network of churches that I and a team of other leaders oversee, has broadened our scope to include micro church networks. Our experience prior to this has been mostly with small groups in a megachurch and small groups in community churches. However, we realize that small group-based community churches, small group-based megachurches and micro church networks, although different, are close cousins.

In light of this, we are adding specific training to our current leadership training school for micro church planters. Brian Sauder, director of the school, emphasizes that "there can be small groups in micro churches, small groups in community churches and small groups in megachurches. If we want all three types of churches to coexist, we will need to be proactive in training for all three." Through the DOVE Global Leadership & Ministry School, hundreds of leaders both locally and around the world (through the online arm of the school) have been trained. Learn more at https://dcfi.org/ministry-school/.

We want to stay current with what the Lord is doing. We believe we are called by the Lord to help start new small group-based community churches, small group-based megachurches, and small group-based micro churches that form micro church networks, because all of these are part of the Lord's plan for His church. Leaders of all denominations and movements should be prudent to reach out to those within their family of churches and help them start micro church networks, lest future micro church leaders within their denominations look elsewhere for spiritual oversight.

My friend Mike Bickle, Director of International House of Prayer in Kansas City, has often shared that God had revealed to him that "God is going to change the forms and expressions of church within one generation to a great degree." He has expressed that "the house church network is a vital ingredient in that change."

In 2 Kings 4:1-7 the story is told of Elisha miraculously multiplying the oil of a poor widow. As long as the widow had vessels to pour the oil into, the flow of oil continued. But when she ran out of vessels, the supply of new oil was halted. In many ways, this story is a prophetic picture of the purpose of God for the church. He has promised to pour out His Holy Spirit in these last days, but this will necessitate flexible containers to hold the great harvest that is on the horizon. Is it possible that the Lord is waiting for His church to prepare the proper containers so He can fully pour out His Spirit?

The challenge before us

Now is the time to prepare leaders for the coming harvest. We cannot force new Christians into our old wineskins—we must prepare new wineskins for the new wine. Forming new vessels will facilitate the Lord's commission to make disciples. Many new types of vessels, including new micro churches networking together in our communities, are needed.

I have felt the Lord impressing me that He is giving His people an invitation. He says in His Word, "Ask me, and I will make the nations your inheritance, the ends of the earth your possession" (Psalm 2:8). I am convinced that God is inviting many of us to ask Him for laborers for His harvest, and to partner together with others to plant new micro churches in our communities, our regions, our nation, and in the nations of the world.

Let's get about our Father's business and partner together with the body of Christ for kingdom expansion.

Questions Most
Often Asked About
Micro Church Networks

What is the difference between a micro church and a small group-based church?

There is a big difference between a micro church and a small group-based church. Micro churches are self-contained churches in themselves; they are not just home groups within a wider church structure. The small group-based community churches or megachurches, however, usually have their own headquarters with an administrative structure. Micro churches require no headquarters; they are much more flexible and fluid because they meet solely in homes or other places (coffee shops, offices, etc.) and do not require another building for further church programs.

In small group-based community churches and megachurches, the small group leaders are an extension of the leadership of the elders of the local church where believers meet each Sunday in a larger gathering. Micro churches are entire churches by themselves. Each micro church has elders who serve as fathers and mothers and have a heart's cry to train and reproduce more leaders within the micro church. Micro churches also may have a few small satellite groups to help disciple new believers and give hands-on training for future micro church leaders.

The micro church models a way of life. It takes place entirely outside of the mentality of religious meetings. Church becomes people living their lives in an extended spiritual family as they focus on reaching the lost. Although families require some organization, it is a relational organization, minus the bureaucracy.

What if a micro church is not a part of a micro church network?

The reason for micro church networks is to provide accountability and encouragement to individual micro churches. Exclusiveness is unhealthy for a micro church. Every micro church really should be connected to others in some way.

What is the difference between a community church, a megachurch and a micro church network?

A community church (a church of between fifty to one thousand people meeting in a building) and megachurch (generally a church of over one or two thousand) function largely within traditional church structures. They meet in church buildings every Sunday morning and may or may not have small groups meeting in homes during the week. The community church reaches out to its local community and can be compared to a neighborhood store, which has a similar scope of influence. The megachurch, however, could be compared to the Walmart superstore because it reaches a wider area. People in megachurches often travel longer distances to attend meetings, which offer a broad range of services.

The micro church networks are entirely different from the community and megachurches because each gathering of believers is a church in itself with its own elders and leadership. These micro church networks are like the average stores in a shopping mall because each church needs to network with others in order to flourish. They meet as a church in homes or other locations that do not require construction of a dedicated building that can accommodate a larger group. They focus on growing by starting new micro churches.

Could some community churches or megachurches adopt micro churches?

All three kinds of churches can help to disciple people and change lives. Some community churches and megachurches will commission leaders to start micro churches. Some community church and megachurch leaders will give them the oversight needed to help them grow.

Other community churches and megachurches will "adopt" micro churches in their communities and help them network together.

Could some community churches or megachurches become micro churches?

Even though most micro churches will continue to birth new micro churches, some micro churches may actually become community churches. And some of these community churches could become megachurches. There is tremendous freedom in the kingdom of God!

Which of these three kinds of churches is best?

All three! It just depends on which one you are called to. God will use whichever structure He chooses, and He does not necessarily ask us for our opinion. As soon as we think our group is the only "right" group, we get in trouble. Pride always comes before a fall. We must, with great conviction, follow the path the Lord has laid out for us, but honor what He is doing through others who are doing it differently than we are.

Do we need leadership in micro churches and micro church networks?

Yes. Servant leadership, fatherly leadership, but always some form of godly leadership. If God's appointed leader does not give proper leadership, then the enemy will be sure someone else, who is not God's appointed leader, does. The Bible is filled with examples of team leadership with primary leadership among the team. Leaders are necessary.

Will every young believer get involved in a micro church network?

No, many young people will be called by the Lord to serve in community churches while others serve in megachurches. But many young believers today will get involved in micro church networks because this expression of church seems to correspond with the value system of their generation.

What about children in micro churches?

The Lord values children. They can take an active role in micro church life because they are part of the spiritual family. There are many creative options for children. Some micro churches keep the children with them the entire time. Other micro churches have the children involved with their parents for about half of the meeting, then someone in the micro church ministers to the children in other room for the rest of the time.

What are some pitfalls and traps to avoid in micro church networks?

A common pitfall and trap to avoid in micro churches and micro church networks is pride. Micro churches are not the cure-all for today's ailing church. If those of us who are called to micro church networks take a superior attitude, the Bible tells us we will fall. Another pitfall to avoid is fear. We must learn to move in faith, not in fear. A further pitfall is developing an independent and isolationist spirit. Micro churches may also fall into the pitfall of heresy if they are exclusive and unwilling to work with others.

How should those of us called to community churches or megachurches respond to micro church networks in our community?

Let's welcome them, reach out to them and offer to help them succeed. We must allow micro church networks to grow up alongside the community churches and megachurches in our communities and realize we are all a part of the regional church the Lord is raising up.

Could you tell me what a healthy micro church network is not?

First of all, a healthy micro church is not made up of people who are disgruntled with the community church or megachurch. Second, a healthy micro church is not an ingrown club of people who have forgotten the harvest. Third, it is not Christians who are independent and unwilling to submit to the recognized leaders within the body of

Christ because they do not believe in spiritual authority. Fourth, healthy micro church networks are not groups of people who have been together for a number of years and have only slightly grown in size or have not grown at all.

How does the micro church network fit into the regional church the Lord is restoring in geographical regions of the world?

More and more leaders from all types of churches are realizing the need for healthy relationships among different churches in a community. The micro church network fits the regional church like a hand in a glove since it is just another form of church. The only way it will not fit is if the micro churches become independent and refuse to work with anyone else or if the existing churches do not accept micro churches.

What is DOVE International?

DOVE International started with a group of young Christian believers who had a burden to reach out in love to the unchurched youth in their local community in northern Lancaster County, Pennsylvania.

It was the early 1970s and a time of a nationwide awakening among young people in the United States. The nation had been through tumultuous times in the 1960s with rapid changes tearing at the fabric of our society, including the sexual revolution, Vietnam War, and abortion rights. After a decade in which many young people were dabbling in the occult and drug culture seeking answers for life, but ending up disillusioned, they were now turning to God in great numbers.

Christian song writers and screenwriters were producing songs like, I Wish We'd All Been Ready. A movie entitled A Thief in the Night described possible end-time scenarios. These and other notable trends jolted Christian young people from their complacency. Many of these young people developed a genuine burden for their world, because the end seemed near.

It was in these times that a group of Christian young people living in south central Pennsylvania, started an organization called "The Lost But Found." Through friendship evangelism, we saw many young people come to know Jesus as their Lord. A Bible study under the direction of Larry Kreider called "Rhema Youth Ministries" nurtured many of these young Christians.

New wineskins for the new wine

Although we tried to get them involved, the new believers to whom we were relating simply didn't fit into the established churches in our community. It seemed clear there was a need for new church structures flexible enough to relate to new converts from a variety of backgrounds. That's why Jesus said we need to put new wine into new wineskins: "Nor do they put new wine into old wineskins, or else the wineskins break, the wine is spilled, and the wineskins are ruined. But they put new wine into new wineskins, and both are preserved" (Matthew 9:16-17).

There was an increasing need for a flexible New Testament-style church (new wineskin) that could relate to and assist these new believers (new wine) in their spiritual growth. In 1978, God spoke to Larry Kreider about being "willing to be involved with the underground church."

Our adventure into small groups

So began our church's adventure into small groups. A small group was started in Larry and LaVerne Kreider's home. When their living room was filled to capacity, they turned over the group to leaders they had trained and started a second group in another home. The roots began to grow for an "underground church" where believers were nourished in these "underground" small groups as they gathered to pray, evangelize and build relationships with each other. We believed when the underground roots (individuals in relationship in small groups) are healthy, the whole church would be strong.

By the time DOVE Christian Fellowship officially began in October, 1980, there were approximately twenty-five believers meeting in a large living room on Sunday mornings and in three small groups during the week. In the small groups, people had the opportunity to experience and demonstrate Christianity built on relationships, not simply on meetings. In the small groups, people could readily share their lives with each other and reach out with the healing love of Jesus to a broken world. The desire was to follow the pattern in the New Testament church as modeled in the book of Acts, as the believers met from house to house.

Twelve years later, as these small groups continued to grow and to multiply, more than 2,300 believers were meeting in over 125 small groups all over south central Pennsylvania. Churches were planted in Scotland, Brazil, Kenya, and New Zealand. Believers met in small groups in homes during the week and in clusters of small groups in geographical areas for celebration meetings each Sunday morning to worship together, receive teaching and celebrate what the Lord was doing during the week through the small groups. Every few months the entire church would meet together to worship on a Sunday morning in a large gymnasium or in a local park.

Several times, Sunday celebration meetings were halted for a four-week period and small groups met on Sunday mornings. This was intended to strengthen the vision for building the church underground. During one of those times, the Lord added one hundred people to the church by the time Sunday celebration meetings resumed.

We made our share of mistakes

Although the church had grown rapidly in a relatively short span, we made our share of mistakes. The Lord began to deal with pride and unhealthy control in our lives. We found the Lord's purpose for small groups was to release and empower His people, not to control them. We repented before the Lord and before His church.

Our small group-based church had reached a crossroads. We were experiencing the pain of gridlock among some of our leaders. There was an exodus of some good leaders from our ranks. It was painful. Larry Kreider, who was serving as the senior pastor, almost quit.

In retrospect, we feel the mistakes we made were partly due to our immaturity as leaders and partly due to not having an outside accountability team to help us when we ran into conflicts in decision-making. Perhaps the Lord in His providence was repositioning some of His players elsewhere in the body of Christ.

But the Lord kept taking us back to the original vision He had given, calling us to be involved with the "underground church." Today we walk with a spiritual limp, but we are so grateful to the Lord for what He taught us during those days.

Transition

It became clear that in order for DOVE (an acronym for "Declaring Our Victory Emmanuel") to accomplish what we were originally called to accomplish, we needed to adjust our church government and "give the church away." The vision the Lord had given us, "to build a relationship with Jesus, with one another, and reach the world from house to house, city to city and nation to nation," could not be fulfilled through the church structure we were using. We recognized the Lord had called us to be an apostolic movement, but we did not know how it should be structured.

It took more than two years to prepare for this transition. On January 1, 1996, our church in the USA became eight individual churches, each with their own elder team. We formed an Apostolic Council to give spiritual oversight to DOVE, and Larry Kreider was asked to serve as its International Director. The Apostolic Council gave each church elder team of these churches the option of becoming a part of the DOVE family of churches and ministries or connecting to another part of the body of Christ. Each of these eight churches expressed a desire to become part of the DOVE family and work together to plant churches throughout the world. The majority of the overseas church plants also desired to become a part of the DOVE family of churches and ministries.

We have found apostolic ministry provides a safe environment for each congregation and ministry partnering with DOVE to grow and reproduce themselves. This new model emphasizes leading by relationship and influence rather than hands-on-management. A lead elder and team (we prefer to call the leader of a congregation a lead elder, rather than senior pastor, simply because he may or may not have the actual gift of a pastor) have a leadership gift to equip believers to do the work of ministry. The Apostolic Council members are responsible to spend time in prayer and the ministry of the Word and give training, oversight and mentoring to local church leadership. They also are called to give clear vision and direction to the entire movement.

Becoming an apostolic movement

Unlike an "association of churches," which gives ordination and general accountability to church leaders, we see an "apostolic movement" as a family of churches with a common focus—a mandate from God to labor together to plant and establish churches throughout the world. Although some may call us a new denomination, we prefer the terminology "apostolic movement" or "international family of churches."

We do not mind being called a denomination, but denominationalism often separates us rather than focus on our need for the Lord and for each other. We believe each denomination and movement has a redemptive purpose from God, and we need to honor, serve and learn from each other. We build on the shoulders of those who have gone on before us.

As a church planting movement, we are intent on training a new generation of church planters and leaders just waiting for a chance to spread their wings and fly! We are called to mobilize and empower God's people (individuals, families, small groups, congregations, and micro church networks) at the grassroots level to fulfill His purposes. Every small group should have a vision to plant new groups. Every church should have a God-given vision to plant new churches.

Partnering together

For many years, we knew we were called to plant new churches, but a few years ago, the Lord spoke to Larry, "I have many orphans in my body, and I am calling you to adopt some of my orphans." God was calling us to also open our hearts to churches who had no spiritual oversight and apostolic protection. Now, in addition to church planting and multiplication, we have defined a process for adopting churches who are called to partner with us. After going through a one-year engagement process of discernment, churches with similar values and vision became partner churches in the DOVE family.

Our transition from one church into several churches has allowed the old structure to die so we could experience the new—a network of churches partnering together. At the time of this writing, there are over one thousand churches and ministries either in the engagement period or partnering with the DOVE family from nations in six continents of the world. Each DOVE partner church is governed by a team of elders and consists of believers committed to one another in small groups. Each church has its own identity while being interdependent with the rest of the DOVE family.

Our desire is to see congregations of small groups and micro churches clustered together in the same area so leaders can easily meet as regional presbyteries and find ways to be more effective in building His kingdom together. Lead elders of DOVE churches in Pennsylvania have the blessing of meeting together each month for prayer and mutual encouragement. This same pattern is encouraged in other regions where DOVE partner churches are in close proximity to one another. Apostolic leaders provide further oversight and accountability to the lead elders.

The need for new wineskins once again

A few years ago, we noticed that today's generation was feeling a similar stirring to what we felt in our younger days. They craved a new type of wineskin that would provide a more contemporary venue for church life. They were saying the same kind of things we had said years earlier: "We are looking for something new. We need something that truly meets our needs." Our wineskin had begun to age—it was past its prime for many of the younger generation.

It didn't take long to conclude that we must find ways to plant new churches (new wineskins) and begin the process of handing over the reins to the next generation. We encouraged the young people to start something new—a new kind of church for a new generation. Today there are various micro church networks established in the DOVE family in the USA and around the world.

Our micro churches have small groups for training new leaders that give every believer the opportunity to minister. Instead of constructing a church building when a house or place they are meeting in is outgrown, a new micro church is planted. Dr. Peter Wagner has said so often, "The single most effective method of evangelism is to plant new churches."

Networking with the body of Christ

We believe another important aspect to kingdom building is networking with other churches and ministries outside of the DOVE family. In this way, we can resource one other. We welcome the exchange of Christian leaders between the DOVE apostolic movement and others in the body of Christ as we learn from the rest of God's family and share what the Lord has given to us. DOVE partner church leaders are encouraged to pray regularly with other pastors and participate in pastors' gatherings in their regions.

God has given us wonderful support teams including the DOVE International Apostolic Council, more than forty regional apostolic teams (overseeing churches on five continents), a team of Fivefold Translocal Ministers, a Stewardship Council (handling the administration of financial details and legalities), and various ministries that are committed to resource the leadership and believers in DOVE partner churches and serve the greater body of Christ.

These various ministries offer leadership training and ministry development on many levels. An essential twenty-four-hour Prayer Ministry includes a team of "prayer generals" who recruit, train and encourage a team of "prayer warriors" responsible to cover segments of time each week while praying for the entire DOVE family twenty-four hours a day.

The International Apostolic Council and leadership from DOVE partner churches throughout the world meet together for an annual DOVE International Leadership Conference for the purpose of mutual encouragement, leadership training, relationship building, and to receive a common vision from the Lord. DOVE partner church leaders also gather each year regionally and/or nationally for strategic prayer, relationship building, leadership training and mutual encouragement. We believe the Lord has called us to build together through relationships and work as a team—with a shared vision, shared biblical values and shared procedure.

In order for the DOVE family of churches and ministries to be effective in laboring together, we wrote our procedure, including constitution and by-laws, in a handbook. This *DOVE International Leadership Handbook* is available by contacting the DOVE office at 717.627.1996 or can be found at info@dcfi.org.

Training and releasing God's people

An important philosophy of ministry at DOVE is to release each believer and local leadership team in order to provide a delegation of authority and responsibility to all believers. Unless elders release responsibility and authority to the small group leaders, this principle will not work. In this way, the Lord releases every believer to be a minister.

Every church leader is encouraged to maintain a sense of security in the Lord and take the risk of empowering and releasing small group leaders to minister to others as they perform water baptisms, serve communion, pray for the sick, give premarital counseling, and disciple new believers. A major aspect of small group ministry is preparing and training future spiritual fathers and mothers. Many of these leaders will be future elders and church planters as they experience on-the-job training.

Various training schools are available through DOVE. The DOVE Global Leadership & Ministry School is an online comprehensive ministry training school of 216 twenty-minute classes that can be completed on your phone or computer anywhere in the world.

The philosophy in the DOVE family is to train individuals so they can be given away to start their own spiritual families—new small groups and new churches that they plant.

Fivefold trans-local ministry

According to Ephesians 4:11-12, persons who flow in the five ministry gifts of the apostle, prophet, evangelist, pastor and teacher are called by the Lord to equip the saints to minister and encourage the body of Christ. Within the DOVE family, fivefold ministers who have proven ministries are recommended by their elders as having a larger sphere of ministry than their own small group and local church. They are also recognized and affirmed by the Apostolic Council in their region of the world to serve trans-locally. These trans-local ministers are often invited by other small groups and local churches for ministry.

DOVE mission outreaches

DOVE has sent hundreds of short and long-term missionaries to the nations. Each long-term missionary is "embraced" by a small group, a local church, and by individuals from DOVE partner churches. A team of people joins a missionary's support team by giving financially and praying for the missionary. Small groups who "embrace" a missionary or missionary family pray for them, write to them, and serve the missionary practically while on furlough or during times of crisis.

DOVE Mission International endeavors to serve all DOVE missionaries who are sent out from DOVE partner churches regardless of which "field" they serve in. Some missionaries are directly involved in the DOVE church planting "field," while others may serve instead with YWAM or with some other mission agency. We are called to build the kingdom, not just our own network of churches. Yet, as a network of churches, we are called by the Lord as a spiritual family to plant new churches together in the unreached areas of the world.

We currently have three DOVE Mission centers that are responsible for training and releasing missionaries: one in Pennsylvania, USA, one in Nairobi, Kenya and one in Keswick, Ontario.

The vision continues

The Bible tells us that without a vision the people perish. The DOVE family is called to stay actively involved in what the Lord is doing in the world and participate in the present expressions of His anointing. We desire to empower, train, and release God's people at the grassroots level to fulfill His purposes. Jesus values people. He has called us to see people from the Father's perspective, and see Him working in and through them. Jesus only did what He saw His Father doing, and He calls us to do the same.

In order to most effectively fulfill God's overall purpose for us, we are committed to continuing the wholehearted pursuit of the specific vision and calling that God has given us—to build the church with an "underground" focus in the nations of the world.

Looking unto Jesus, the Lord of the harvest

Like our early beginnings, we are again sensing that the harvest is upon us. The Lord, like a great magnet, is drawing people into His kingdom. Since new wineskins eventually get old, many who have been believers for years are becoming dissatisfied. God's people are again thirsting for new wine and new wineskins. The Lord is renewing, refreshing and reviving thousands of His people all over the world. He is requiring us to provide new wineskins for the new wine as He brings in His harvest.

We need to continue to commune with the Lord daily and obey His voice. Every generation is different and has diverse needs and preferences. We are committed to empowering, releasing, and supporting the next generations among us as they fulfill their call in God. As Elisha received a double portion of Elijah's anointing, we want to see our spiritual children far exceeding us in their depth of spiritual experience and church leadership.

APPENDIX C

Recommended Reading

Brian Sanders and Mark Patz, *Different: Reimagining Holiness for a Wandering Church in a Watching World* (Tampa, FL: Underground Media, 2014).

Brian Sanders, *Underground Church: A Living Example of the Church in its Most Potent Form* (Grand Rapids, MI: Zondervan, 2018).

Dean Briggs, *Ekklesia Rising: The Authority of Christ in Communities of Contending Prayer* (Kansas City, MO: Champion Press, 2014).

Deitrich Bonhoeffer, *Life Together*, Translated by David W. Bloesch (Minneapolis, MN: Fortress Press, 2015).

Ed Silvoso, *Ekklessia: Rediscovering God's Instrument for Global Transformation* (Bloomington, MN: Chosen Books, 2014, 2017).

Larry Kreider, *House to House: Growing Healthy Small Groups and House Churches in the 21st Century* (Lititz, PA: House to House Publications, 2008).

Larry Kreider, *The Cry for Spiritual Mothers and Fathers* (Bloomington, MN: Chosen Books, 2014).

Larry Kreider and Floyd McClung, *Starting a House Church* (Ventura, CA: Regal Books, 2007).

Larry Kreider, Ron Myer, Steve Prokopchak, Brian Sauder, *The Biblical Role of Elders for Today's Church* (Lititz, PA: DOVE International, 2019).

Mark Perry, *Kingdom Churches: New Strategies for a Revival Generation* (Arroyo Grande, CA: Cameo Books, 2015).

Peter Bunton, *Cell Groups and House Churches: What History Teaches Us* (Lititz, PA: House to House Publications, 2001).

Ralph Moore, *Making Disciples: Developing Lifelong Followers of Jesus* (Grand Rapids, MI: Baker Books, 2012).

Ron Myer, *Fivefold Ministry Made Practical* (Lititz, PA: House to House Publications, 2006).

Steve Addison, *Movements that Change the World* (Downers Grove, IL: Inter-Varsity Press, 2011).

Steve Addison, *Pioneering Movements* (Downers Grove, IL: Inter-Varsity Press, 2015).

Steve Addison, *The Rise and Fall of Movements* (100Movements Publishing, 2019).

Steve Addison, *What Jesus Started: Joining a Movement and Changing the World* (Downer's Grove, IL: Inter-Varsity Press, 2012).

DOVE GLOBAL
LEADERSHIP & MINISTRY SCHOOL
[ONLINE]

PAY LESS
FOR **ONLINE LEADERSHIP & MINISTRY TRAINING**

- Dynamic online video training in ministry and leadership

- Learn at your own pace – 20 minutes per class

- 216 classes taught by a broad spectrum of seasoned leaders

- Access the content from anywhere in the world on any device

For more info, visit DCFI.org/Online-School

House to House

The church is waking up to the simple, successful house to house strategy practiced by the New Testament church. *House to House* documents how God called a fellowship of believers to become a house to house movement. During the past years, DOVE International has grown into a family of small group based churches and micro churches networking throughout the world. *by Larry Kreider, 264 pages.* **$15.99**

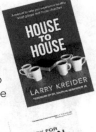

Cry for Spiritual Mothers and Fathers

Returning to the biblical truth of spiritual parenting so believers are not left fatherless and disconnected. How loving, seasoned spiritual fathers and mothers help spiritual children reach their full potential in Christ. *by Larry Kreider, 224 pages.* **$14.99**

Fivefold Ministry

Discover how the fivefold ministry was created to work within the local church, the training ground for ministry. These ministers-apostles, prophets, evangelists, pastors and teachers-are coaches who equip and train God's people for works of service. Find out what the fivefold ministry is and what it is not as we learn how proven ministers can be released in the body of Christ. *by Ron Myer, 208 pages.* **$15.99**

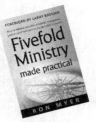

Cell Groups and House Churches: What History Teaches Us

A historical backdrop to much of what is happening in cell groups and house churches today. Explore the writings and practices of the Reformers such as Luther and Bucer, as well as the Pietists, Moravians, Methodists and others. *by Peter Bunton, 108 pages.* **$9.99**

The Biblcal Role of Elders for Today's Church

Healthy leadership teams produce healthy churches! New Testament principles for equipping church leadership teams: What are the qualifications and responsibilities, how elders should be chosen, how elders function as spiritual fathers and mothers, how elders should make decisions, resolve conflicts and more. Included are questionnaires for evaluating a team of elders. by Larry Kreider, Ron Myer, Steve Prokopchak, and Brian Sauder, 274 pages. **$12.99**

Straight Talk to Leaders

What we wish we had known when we started. Four Christian leaders disclose key leadership lessons they have learned through forty years of pastoring and establishing worldwide ministries. This illuminating book explores topics such as team building, boundaries, transitions, unity, stress management, learning from criticism, making tough decisions and much more! *by Larry Kreider, Sam Smucker, Barry Wissler and Lester Zimmerman, 204 pages.* **$12.99**

Passing the 21 Tests of Leadership

Whether you are called to lead in business, your community or church, life is filled with tests! Will you be able to pass them? *"I encourage every believer who desires to reach his or her maximum leadership potential to invest in this book."* - *Robert Stearns, Eagles' Wings Ministries.* by Larry Kreider, 218 pages. **$16.99**

Biblical Foundation Series

This series by Larry Kreider covers basic Christian doctrine. Practical illustrations accompany the easy-to-understand format. Use for small group teachings (48 in all), a mentoring relationship or daily devotional. Each book has 64 pages: **$5.99** each, 12 Book Set: **$39** Also available in Spanish and French.

Biblical Foundation Titles
1. Knowing Jesus Christ as Lord
2. The New Way of Living
3. New Testament Baptisms
4. Building For Eternity
5. Living in the Grace of God
6. Freedom from the Curse
7. Learning to Fellowship with God
8. What is the Church?
9. Authority and Accountability
10. God's Perspective on Finances
11. Called to Minister
12. The Great Commission

MANY DISCOUNTS!

House To House Publications
1.800.848.5892
Online: www.h2hp.com
email: H2HP@dcfi.org